Praise for *When God Rescripts Your Life*

"Jaci's recollections of her life are worth reading for two reasons: she doesn't sugarcoat the gritty details—which is a good payoff for a curious reader—and in telling her story, she finds the wonder and mystery of God's endless ability to turn our chaos into beauty."

—AMY GRANT

"What I have always loved about Jaci Velasquez is that she's 100 percent herself—confident, bubbly, kind, earnest. There's always been a fearlessness about Jaci's presence, a willingness to be vulnerable and real. In *When God Rescripts Your Life*, Jaci pours her story onto the page, offering honest, hopeful, sometimes humorous reflections on navigating life's unexpected surprises. Like her music, Jaci's story will encourage you, help you feel less alone, and remind you how God uses life's challenges to help us see what's true, what's important, and what's beautiful about the journey."

—MATTHEW PAUL TURNER, AUTHOR OF *WHEN I PRAY FOR YOU* AND *WHEN GOD MADE YOU*

"Life doesn't always go as planned—as we planned. But God always has a greater purpose. Jaci Velasquez's *When God Rescripts Your Life* is a beautiful example of this. Her intricate story reveals how God is always at work, revealing himself to us in both the ordinary and extraordinary. After reading Jaci's insightful and inspiring story, I am encouraged and ready to 'flip the script' in my own life and trust God with my dreams."

—SANDI PATTY, SINGER, AUTHOR, MOST AWARDED FEMALE VOCALIST IN GOSPEL HISTORY

"*When God Rescripts Your Life* is a must-read. You won't be able to put this book down. The journey that this book takes you through will have you smiling, laughing, crying, praying, and thanking God for those unknown adventures that we often face. This incredible book provides fresh insight on how to handle life's curve balls. Sometimes you have to let go of the pen and let God do the rescripting."

—DESTINY MARKO, WORSHIP PASTOR OF EVANGEL CHURCH

"I love how God is able to turn what we consider messes into a master-piece. That's what he has done in my life and in the life of Jaci! I am so thrilled to celebrate and recommend Jaci's new book. I believe that it will be a true inspiration and encouragement in your life!"
—NICOLE C MULLEN, SINGER, SONGWRITER, AND CHOREOGRAPHER

"In *When God Rescripts Your Life*, Jaci Velasquez candidly shares about her family, career, and faith— her life. She pulls back the curtain and shares everything she's been through that has brought her to where she is today. Her story will encourage and equip readers to trust God through the ups and downs of life, knowing he has a greater purpose and plan."
—MARK SCHULTZ, PLATINUM-SELLING AND DOVE
AWARD-WINNING RECORDING ARTIST

"I love how Jaci has so beautifully shared her journey with all of us, and that she discovered the difference between a God-given dream and her own. Though she's been through great challenges, she's seen great personal triumph. In her always sweet and relatable style, she perfectly communicates the important understanding that God often 'flips the script' we've written for ourselves into one that proves far more mean-ingful over time. I'm so proud of Jaci and have really enjoyed this book and I know you will too! Prepare to be inspired and encouraged to find the script God has written for your life."
—LORI CROUCH, HOST OF TRINITY BROADCASTING NETWORK

"There are two words I would use to describe this book: *helpful truth.* Some books give you information but it's not transformative. Other books seek to help, but the basis is personal opinion and not much else. Jaci manages to accomplish both. The book will connect with real issues and you will see real intervention from a real God. I recommend it to anyone to is tired of clichés and seeks to experience real transfor-mation. God sometimes allows temporary pain to produce permanent blessings, and this book captures that process."
—ROGER HERNANDEZ, AUTHOR, SPEAKER FOR SU CONFERENCE
OF SDA, AND MINISTERIAL AND EVANGELISM DIRECTOR

"Jaci takes us on a journey of highs and lows that draw us into beauty. With a desire to seek truth, the promises of God have secured a place of true peace in her life. As a musician, actress, wife, and mother she has found that God continues to work in ways higher than her own, and she encourages us to continually be on the lookout for the same."

—DAVID LEONARD, PRODUCER, WRITER,
AND MUSICIAN ON THE JOURNEY

"Jaci lets you into her very private and personal pain to give hope to anyone who has ever had life not turn out quite how you planned. Beauty from ashes."

—PLUMB, RECORDING ARTIST AND AUTHOR

"*When God Rescripts Your Life* is a powerful, life-changing read for anyone who has ever felt abandoned by God. Jaci Velasquez shares her fascinating life story in such a candid, honest, and humorous way that you'll find yourself laughing, crying, and nodding along with every page. As a fellow member of the "Moms of Kids Who Don't Fit the Script We Wrote" tribe, I found her raw honesty about her journey to acceptance strikingly powerful. And I found incredible comfort and inspiration in the way she effortlessly relates modern day challenges to biblical experiences. She brings those ancient stories to life, highlighting how they are relevant and powerfully inspirational today. If you, like me, ever questioned God's wisdom or love in the face of overwhelming life challenges, I highly recommend this book. Through Jaci's lens, you'll discover that the script you didn't envision—the one God wrote for you—is actually infinitely more beautiful and meaningful than the one you wrote for yourself."

—WENDY TUCKER-WING, FRIEND AND FELLOW
MOM OF A CHILD WITH SPECIAL NEEDS

"Anyone looking for inspiration to get back up, chase their dreams, and renew their faith will treasure this book and its life transforming understandings."

—RUDY PEREZ, AWARD-WINNING ARTIST,
PRODUCER, COMPOSER, AND AUTHOR

"Jaci not only shares her personal story, but also poses questions and strategies to help us learn to trust the Lord with the interruptions that occur in our own lives."

—RANDY PHILLIPS OF PHILLIPS, CRAIG AND DEAN

When God
Rescripts
YOUR LIFE

When God
Rescripts
YOUR LIFE

Seeing Value, Beauty, and Purpose
When Life Is Interrupted

JACI VELASQUEZ
WITH JULIE LYLES CARTER

NELSON
BOOKS

An Imprint of Thomas Nelson

Published in Nashville, Tennessee, by Nelson Books, an imprint of Thomas Nelson. Nelson Books and Thomas Nelson are registered trademarks of HarperCollins Christian Publishing, Inc.

Author is represented by the literary agency of The Fedd Agency, Inc., P.O. Box 341973, Austin, Texas, 78734.

Thomas Nelson titles may be purchased in bulk for educational, business, fund-raising, or sales promotional use. For information, please e-mail SpecialMarkets@ThomasNelson.com.

Unless otherwise noted, Scripture quotations are taken from the Holy Bible, New International Version®, NIV®. Copyright © 1973, 1978, 1984, 2011 by Biblica, Inc.® Used by permission of Zondervan. All rights reserved worldwide. www.Zondervan.com. The "NIV" and "New International Version" are trademarks registered in the United States Patent and Trademark Office by Biblica, Inc.®

Scripture quotations marked THE MESSAGE are from The Message. Copyright © by Eugene H. Peterson 1993, 1994, 1995, 1996, 2000, 2001, 2002. Used by permission of NavPress. All rights reserved. Represented by Tyndale House Publishers, Inc.

Scripture quotations marked NCV are from the New Century Version®. © 2005 by Thomas Nelson. Used by permission. All rights reserved.

Scripture quotations marked NKJV are from the New King James Version®. © 1982 by Thomas Nelson. Used by permission. All rights reserved.

Scripture quotations marked NRSV are from New Revised Standard Version Bible. Copyright © 1989 National Council of the Churches of Christ in the United States of America. Used by permission. All rights reserved.

Scripture quotations marked TLB are from The Living Bible. Copyright © 1971. Used by permission of Tyndale House Publishers, Inc., Carol Stream, Illinois 60188. All rights reserved.

Any Internet addresses, phone numbers, or company or product information printed in this book are offered as a resource and are not intended in any way to be or to imply an endorsement by Thomas Nelson, nor does Thomas Nelson vouch for the existence, content, or services of these sites, phone numbers, companies, or products beyond the life of this book.

ISBN 978-1-4002-1297-2 (eBook)
ISBN 978-1-4002-1296-5 (HC)
ISBN 978-1-4002-1841-7 (custom)

Library of Congress Control Number: 2019946674

Printed in the United States of America
19 20 21 22 23 LSC 10 9 8 7 6 5 4 3 2 1

For anyone who's ever watched a movie more than once and wished for a different ending.

Contents

One

The Lens of Value

It didn't say "contemporary, modern, clean lines, stylish, twenty-first century."

At. All.

And "contemporary, modern, clean lines, stylish, twenty-first century" is totally my thing.

(Yes, *totally* is something I totally say, in real life, all the time. Judge all you want, but I totally communicate through a mash-up of emojis and vintage Valley girl speak.)

In that delicate geopolitical landscape known as "in-law relations," I knew the right posture to take. Which is how this particular piece of furniture came to live at my house. It was a gift from my mother-in-law, a piece that had meant a lot to her in her early homemaking days, something that she no longer had room for when she moved from Austin, Texas, to Tennessee to be closer to her grandchildren and my husband, Nic, and me.

When your in-laws move halfway across the country from the only city they've ever called home for the sole reason of being closer to you, it's time for a little give. And take. So I took . . . it.

A boxy cabinet set on spindly legs, made of scuffed, scratched, orangey-purple stained wood. Housed inside was an ancient sewing machine, giving off a slight perfume of machine oil from the gears and wheels. At least, I think they're gears and wheels. Herein lies the sum total of my sewing machine expertise: I know what one looks like. The end. How the thing runs and somehow produces slipcovers and pillows is an absolute mystery to me. Really, the whole thing was an orangey-purple alien as far as I was concerned. A whole piece of furniture, completely dedicated to hiding a massively heavy sewing machine? Was this piece of equipment necessary to survive the wilds of family life four or five decades ago? And what was I supposed to do with it now that it had arrived at my house, into my possession, slouching awkwardly against my living room's crisp white wall? It was an interruption in the midst of my white leather sofa and white entertainment system that floated in the middle of my open-concept space, anchored by a black-and-white cowhide rug, a tableau that had zero need for a stitchery sideboard. *The things we do for the love of family.*

I left it dawdling there against the wall for a good long while, not sure what to do with it, equally not sure how I could secret it out of the house and onto the firepit in the backyard. It was out of place in my carefully planned modern decor, the pieces thoughtfully acquired and positioned. For a brief, shining moment, I envisioned it as one of those items someone posts on eBay or Pinterest that ends up being worth some kind of crazy collector money. You've heard of that, right? The very thing someone donates to Goodwill turns out to be worth a cool five hundred bucks. What if this cabinet was something like that, some rare find? For sewing-machine-cabinet collectors. That could be a thing, right?

I did one of those super thorough and completely authoritative Google searches. Nope. I'd only just make enough to ship the thing to the buyer and probably not even enough to do that. Plus, I'd have to figure out the whole eBay thing, and that sounded about as much fun as learning to sew.

Sew, no. And so, no.

The sewing machine cabinet and I were stuck in our dead-end relationship.

•   •   •

Like me, I bet you've inherited some things you would have never chosen. Maybe it's that pile of student loan debt your spouse brought to the marriage. Or that hair-trigger response that pops up whenever someone is being less than truthful. Or that physical trait from your mom that makes it so that no cute pair of jeans ever seems to work on your hips. Or maybe it's a backyard full of chickens, but I'm totally getting ahead of myself.

The reality is, there are just some things that show up in our lives and feel like gnats of irritation. Or like elephants of urgency. Big or small, they all share this common song: They are not what we planned. Not what we expected. Not how we would have scripted. Not how we saw life playing out. I've experienced my share.

Like marrying that person I hoped was "the one." And that request, that thing I really thought God was going to do . . . and then he didn't. Having my world turned upside down by the beautiful baby who aced his Apgar score at birth, who had ten fingers and ten toes, only to find out that he had significant development challenges years later when he headed to school. And I totally relate to trying to do the right thing but it all coming out wrong.

My first response to disappointments like these is to ditch whatever it is. If it doesn't fit, doesn't make sense, then I want to deep-six it. Sometimes I'll even make it super spiritual, praying for it to be cast out of my "garden," proclaiming all kinds of promises.

I've tried dragging any number of those things out to the fire-pit, ready to get them out of the living room of my life. But some of those unexpected things, once they've come through the door of my life, won't squeeze back out no matter how much pushing and pleading I do. They seem to have shown up for a reason. And now I'm going to have to figure out how to make them fit. No matter what I expected, those things require a rescript of my life and where I thought I was headed.

• • •

Where are my girlfriends who like to plan? The ones who gather their ideas and pull out their calendars and create a mental model of how things are going to roll out, whether it's a wedding, a baby shower, a job trajectory, a life?

If you raised your hand, we have that in common. We are the women who get things done. See a need and meet a need, whether it's a project at our kids' schools or a business idea that needs some fuel. While I love a good adventure and I sometimes find a thrill in not knowing exactly what's around the corner, I usually like to see what's around the bend. I want to know what's on the horizon for my boys at school. I find reassurance and constancy in every Friday night being family pizza night in our jammies at the house. Sure, I want a little wiggle room for some creativity, but overall I like things to make sense, events to happen when they're supposed to, and well-laid schedules to roll out just like I planned.

And every now and then, they do.

But there have been plenty of situations in my life that didn't get the memo. They came crashing in at unexpected times. Presented challenges I didn't feel prepared to take on. They were seemingly pointless to me, with about as much use in my life as, say, a random sewing machine in a big, unattractive cabinet— something I had no time or space to deal with.

You've experienced them too. The small things like your car battery being dead when you're trying to get to work in the morning. The big things like the breakup with that guy you just knew you were going to marry.

You've got questions. Why things went the way they did. How you're supposed to put it all back together. Why all your effort and prayer and devising now reads more like some ironic wish list.

And for us planners, it's especially challenging. Our plans become our scripts, and we like things to go according to script. We like knowing our "lines," being able to anticipate how we think our lives will play out. So when things go "off-script," as they say in the acting business, when life seems to go all improv on us, it can make us feel dizzy. Confused. And a little crazy. But those things that take us off-script, those challenges and unexpected messes, well, I haven't yet found a paper planner or smart phone app, organizing blog or Pinterest pin that can remove those obstacles from my life.

But I have met a Maker who has some ideas. A Creator who is very, very good at taking the unexpected, the unwanted, the unwarranted, the unanticipated, the unforeseen and somehow changing them into the elements of an amazing story—a powerful life. He doesn't promise convenience, preferred time schedules, or tidiness. Frankly, he sometimes reminds me of the cable or appliance repair guy who, rather than giving me a specific appointment time to make repairs, just asks me to hang around all day and he'll get there. Eventually.

And *he does.*

The longer I hang around God, the more I'm getting to know him as a particular kind of specialist. Yes, he is the Great Physician, as the heading in my Bible says over that passage in Matthew where Jesus is talking about the sick needing a doctor. But God has also shown me that he's all about eye exams. He is the Great Optometrist, if you will, ready with a series of lenses for me to try out.

Eye exams always crack me up. There's something so weird about sitting on one side of that metal face mask, that thing that looks like a parking meter on steroids suspended in front of my face. The eye doctor sits on the other side, breathing my air. He's so . . . in my face. No one gets their face that close to my face except for Nic and my boys. Then there's the whole sequence of the eye doc flipping through all those various levels of little glass discs in the metal machine, clicking them into place. "This . . . or this?" he asks, the letter chart behind him morphing into greater focus or fuzz with each option. It always startles me, every time he flips to a new disc, my eyelashes brushing against the glass.

"This . . . or this? One . . . or two?" We do this dance for a while, options optically transforming with each click. My brain scrambles to make sense of the latest lens. I try to remember which one seems clearer, the one I'm currently looking through or that one a few clicks ago. And then one more click, and that mush of marks on the far wall is seen through the right lens and

I can read it now. What had looked like ancient hieroglyphs just a moment before, now, with the correct perspective, is something I can recognize, that I can find value for.

This or that?

There is this "eye exam verse" I think about a lot. It was written by Saul, who later became known as Paul, who thought he was doing all kinds of good in the world by trying to make everything predictable, to make it all fit together neatly. It's going to take me a minute to unpack this, so just hang on. When he began to encounter people who were following a radical message of grace from a guy they claimed was not just a messiah but *the* Messiah, Paul sprang into action to shut them down. These people didn't fit with his understanding of how church should be done. This Jesus they were talking about all the time didn't square with how Paul thought God should be doing things. Paul was fired up to protect the status quo, and he went to some extreme measures to try to purge his experience of anything that didn't coordinate with his carefully researched life plan.

So God upped his pursuit of Paul in return and launched a roadside intervention.

Paul was on the road to a town called Damascus, arrest warrants from the high priest in hand, to seek out any of those Jesus people and haul them back to Jerusalem. His plan was all mapped out, he had all the needed paperwork in order, and he was just a few miles away from getting Damascus all reorganized and away from the influence of those unpredictable apostates.

And then a big spotlight showed up and shined right on him, right in the middle of the road. The blinding light engulfed him, and Paul had the unexpected adventure of chatting it up with the very Jesus he was trying to purge from his countrymen.

Paul recounted his experience in Acts 26, and to me it's always felt like Jesus spoke to Paul in some kind of Shakespearean play language. He said, "It is hard for you to kick against the goads" (v. 14). For some reason I hear Jesus saying those words in some Old English accent. But when I dig into that weird phrase, I find something there for you and me.

A goad, or an *oxgoad*, as some of the Bible translations call it, was a wooden stick with a metal point or spike attached to it that was used to keep oxen and cattle in line. It wasn't meant to hurt or abuse the animal, just to give them a nudge as a reminder of the direction their owner wanted them to go. Because when unexpected things happen, oxen will often bolt off, reacting to what has startled them. Sometimes oxen are just flat-out stubborn and want to do their own thing instead of following, and a goad comes in handy—a way for the person responsible for the ox to get this big, blundering animal back into a lane that is best for him. And that's what Paul had been doing. He had been acting like a stubborn ox, kicking against God's best.

So right after Jesus shined the light on Paul and asked why Paul had been persecuting him, Jesus compassionately told him that all that kicking against the goads was injuring him. Paul was actually smashing himself into the very thing that was supposed to lead to a new direction in his life.

And don't miss this: After that conversation, Paul discovered he couldn't see. He'd been blinded by the encounter. He staggered into Damascus, all his plans and paperwork for penalizing Jesus proselytizers in tatters. He landed at the house of Ananias for a few days, and after he was baptized in the name of the very one he was trying to consign to the theological dump, his sight returned.

That's the backstory that leads me to the verse Paul is arguably the most famous for writing. He wrote it a few years after his encounter with Jesus. It's a verse smack in the middle of one of his most famous pieces of writing, that whole Love Chapter in 1 Corinthians 13. He'd been talking about what love is and what it does—that passage you hear at weddings, those words that you'll hear your friends, Christian and non-Christian alike, use when they talk about relationships and selflessness and romance. Paul then pivoted a bit and talked about becoming more mature.

And then he said something about how right now, in this life, we see through a glass darkly.

What? What is this glass and how does one see darkly? (More Shakespearean accent.)

So I dig a little deeper. I like how the New International Version puts it, that we see "only a reflection as in a mirror; then we shall see face to face. Now I know in part; then I shall know fully, even as I am fully known" (1 Cor. 13:12). Now we're getting somewhere.

It's that lens thing again, God as the Great Optometrist. Too often I'm looking into something but I'm not seeing all the way through. I'm only allowing my gaze to bounce back on how this thing is going to impact me, how it reflects on me, how it inconveniences me, how it seems out of step with how I see myself. I'm using what I think is a lens of perspective as a mirror rather than something that sharpens my ability to see and know God. And some of that, just like Paul says, is a now-and-then issue. In my now, in my today, I'm not always going to understand or be able to figure it out; and even if I get greater clarity over time, I'm still not going to fully get all the questions and challenges in this life until I get face-to-face with God.

But that verse still beautifully challenges me. Because all too often I'm using my circumstances as a selfie, looking at things only through my understanding of value, priority, and best wishes.

I don't think it's any mistake that the encounter Paul had

with Jesus on that intended law-enforcement trip on the road to Damascus resulted in him temporarily not being able to use his physical eyes. Paul needed a huge change of perspective, a new set of eyes to navigate a world in which he would learn to follow Jesus.

I need that too. I need to get myself to the Great Eye Doctor on a regular basis and plunk myself down behind his machine of spiritual lenses. I need to learn anew that the lenses I need are not ones that simply bounce back to me how I see things, but rather fresh lenses that I see through all the way to him, with trifocals of trust, grace, and purpose embedded in the optics.

You're not wrong when something shows up in your life and you see it as something that doesn't fit. If it doesn't follow the script, doesn't fit with where you thought you were headed, with how you had dreamed, with what matches the plans and goals you have. You're spot-on. You're right. This challenge or crisis or conundrum, it's okay to notice that it sticks out like the proverbial sore thumb. That's actually the first step: being honest enough to recognize and identify what doesn't fit. But it's confusing. Too often I've tried to "positive think" myself out of really owning that a new challenge in my life isn't positive. I've put on my Pollyanna pigtails and tried to pretend my way out of dealing with the inconvenience or cringe of an unwanted life party crasher careening my way. I've tried ignoring problems and warning signs that popped up on the dashboard of my life, continuing to drive at the same speed, in the same direction, all while emergency lights flashed at me from my peripheral vision.

Goads, if you will.

Here's a revelation for you. (It was for me.)

Ignoring what we don't like in our lives does not make those things invisible. It just puts off the inevitable. And the inevitable is that eventually, one way or another, we're going to have to deal.

Take it from a girl who was varsity level at telling herself there were no weeds in the garden of her life while poison ivy was hanging from every fence.

So being willing to stare down what's shown up and being willing to own that you don't like it are good things.

As long as you don't get stuck there.

Right now, with that challenge, hurt, worry, or fear in your life, go ahead and take a good, hard look at it. Acknowledge that it's there. And realize that you're only seeing the fuzzy outline of it.

Clarity only comes when we put on a new lens.

• • •

So.

Sew.

That sewing machine cabinet. Bulky. An eyesore. Random. No function in my life or living room that I could see. An obstacle to my decor goals. Until I saw it through a different lens.

A corner of our dining room table seemed to collect all the needed bits and trivia of our daily lives. Keys, cell phones, wallets, change, homework to be done. It always bugged me to see all that stuff scattered on the clean, glass-covered white surface of my expansive dining table, an adored statement piece in my modern living area. I needed to create a spot where all those items could live, somewhere accessible but not roaming.

I glanced around the room and saw it with fresh eyes.

That sewing machine cabinet. If I moved it to that spot, on the wall by the back door . . . well, it might just work.

And if I touched it up and gave it a fresh coat of, say, glossy black paint, well then maybe . . .

I was off to Home Depot with a new vision for what could be. I grabbed furniture painting supplies among the plywood-perfumed aisles and headed back to the house. Tarp down, paint can lid off, brush dipped. Stroke by stroke, repurposing began. In under an hour, I'd finished two coats of paint. I stood back to take a look.

I was stunned. The glossy black paint revealed lines on that tacky cabinet I'd not noticed before. The weird spindly legs that I thought looked so disproportional holding up the boxy cabinet? Now I could see the unique turn of the wood, what I would later find out was called a reed leg, with carefully carved grooves to give it dimension. And those simple arched curves that embossed the twin cabinet doors on the front? Where had those come from? Those arcs now gave the front of the cabinet a face, elegant eyebrows above crystal door pulls making for bejeweled eyes. Had those always been there too?

I couldn't wait for the paint to dry to move the sewing cabinet into place to see what it would look like by the back door. When it was just slightly tacky to the touch, I pushed it across the wood floor, still on the paint tarp, to the wall where I hoped it would fit.

And just like that, it practically clicked into place. It fit perfectly in the spot between the expansive picture window framing the view of our backyard and the back door where we come in and out of the house. Just enough wall space on either side to make it look balanced and intentional, not so much wall space that it looked lost or like an afterthought. With its fresh finish and new home, that sewing machine cabinet was now a highlight piece of the room—quirky, unexpected, glamorous, and functional.

It's the perfect spot for dropping keys and school books when we come in the door. It's a great conversation piece, something you can't find in your local home goods store. It makes a statement, its glossy dark paint a dramatic complement to my ice-white walls. It's a thing of honor, a reminder of Nic's childhood and my mother-in-law's generosity.

All because I discovered the beauty of repurposing. All because I embraced the idea of letting something be rescripted. All because one random day, I saw it through the perspective of possibility instead of as a problem.

Now and then I give a little tour of that cabinet to friends who ask about the piece. We talk about the fluted legs and the carving on the front cabinet doors and how heavy the dang thing is, the metal machine still secreted inside. And I show friends the inside of those cabinet doors. In my repurposing of the piece, in my excitement as its beauty was revealed, I didn't get around to painting the inside of those doors, the interior that doesn't show. I suppose a more diligent DIYer would have taken the whole thing apart and carefully sanded and restained and buffed and put it all back together. But I'm glad I didn't. I'm glad that I can show others and remind myself how the whole relationship with this cabinet started for me. How, from our first date, I just didn't think things were going to work out. The inside is still an orangey-purple stained snapshot of where this whole thing started, as an eyesore in my life—up to today, where the power and beauty of repurposing taught me powerful lessons about how to see with fresh eyes.

What is it for you? What's lurking in the living room of your life, unwanted and uninvited? It may be a huge crisis. It may be a small irritant. And you get to choose the lens through which you view it. Through a God lens, you may just discover a way to repurpose that hurt, that failure, that thing that doesn't fit. It could become one of the most functional or helpful things in your life. It could be the seed of you serving others going through something similar. God is all about repurposing the confusing, the mismatched, the seemingly random things that show up in our lives, turning those very things into mission and purpose.

If we're just willing to look.

Flip the Script

: reverse the usual or existing positions in a situation;
do something unexpected or revolutionary.[1]

At the end of each chapter, you'll find a section designed to help you reflect on what you've just read—and some ideas to consider and apply to your life when it comes to the awkward, the unexpected, the unattractive, the unwanted, the confusing. When God is about the business of rescripting things in our lives, we can participate and cooperate in that experience when we are honest about where we thought things were headed, aware of how it actually went down, and open to allowing God to use it in a fresh way.

- Acknowledge it. Okay, there it is. Feel the feels about it. Don't pretend like it doesn't exist. Stare that thing down and own it.
- Notice the lines of it. I'd been so busy noticing the shocking stain colors on the sewing cabinet that I'd never really taken a look at the overall shape of the thing. That trusted friend and coworker who jarred your whole world when you discovered she'd been gossiping about you behind your back and taking credit for your work? Yes, the orangey-purple injustice and hurt of it is going to hit your heart eyes first.

But back up a couple of steps. Friendship overall has beautiful and meaningful lines in your life. Relationships with others have powerful purpose and treasure. Don't let the tacky finish of one friendship shade you toward connection in general.

- Ask yourself, "What if?" What if this situation has something to teach me? What if this hurdle can make me stronger? What if I come through this with better insight and compassion? What if there is possibility for this thing to be a blessing?

Run those scenarios through your mind, specifically looking for where your experience could help others. Paul, the guy Jesus had to blind in order for him to ultimately see, wrote these words to a church he loved in Corinth in the midst of plenty of unexpected, unpleasant, and unplanned things happening to the people there:

Praise be to the God and Father of our Lord Jesus Christ, the Father of compassion and the God of all comfort, who comforts us in all our troubles, so that we can comfort those in any trouble with the comfort we ourselves receive from God. For just as we share abundantly in the sufferings of Christ, so also our comfort abounds through Christ. If we are distressed, it is for your comfort and salvation; if we are comforted, it is for your comfort, which produces in you patient endurance of the same sufferings we suffer. (2 Cor. 1:3–6)

- Choose the story. It's not about covering it up. It's about rethinking it—reimagining it. How do you want to be able to tell the story of this thing on the other side? As a songwriter I've gathered the stories and emotions and experiences of my life to translate them through rhyme and rhythm in music. And you're doing the same thing in yours, whether you know it or not. Your life, your experiences, your encounters make up your story. The story doesn't happen to us; it flows through us, and we have tremendous power in how we tell it, how we sing it. How about you, my friend? How do you want your life to speak, to sing?

Two

Dreaming New Dreams

I got my education in the back seat of an '85 steel-blue Honda. Blue cloth interior with little cigarette burn holes speckled across the upholstery that had a poor patch job trying to hide the damage. My eyes surveyed those burn marks, looking for patterns and lines between the dots, attempting to make constellations on the cloth, anything to distract me from what I was doing.

Get your mind out of the gutter.

The back seat of that Honda was my homeschool classroom where I really did get my education. It was sometimes also my living room. My dining room. My bedroom. My student lounge. And those cigarette burn holes and their subsequent unfortunate patch job were the work of my older brother, who would occasionally borrow the car and sneak a few cigarettes while he drove.

He'd flick the ashes out the open driver's window and they'd fly back into the back seat, stamping a story of fiery freckles across the upholstery.

When I was nine years old, my mom and dad's music and ministry took us to churches all across the country. At some point, my parents realized I could sing, so they added me to the schedule. We'd pack all our stuff in the trunk of Old Blue, hit the road for the next gig, and spend our days on highways and in cheap diners and in churches big and small.

And I would do school in the back seat, workbooks and textbooks scattered on the floorboard. We had a travel TV/VHS combo, and my mom got curriculum for me that had video teaching to go along with a set of textbooks and worksheets. We'd wedge that travel TV/VHS combo between my parents' front seats with the screen facing back to me, and I'd work on sentence diagramming and multiplication tables and spelling words. Then, when my schoolwork was done for the day, I'd watch movies.

Ah, movies. I'm still a huge cinema fanatic and I can absolutely trace where that comes from. Those days driving all over America to get to the next city, state, and church, movies were my window into what I thought were the "normal" lives of other people.

It was through movies that I began to build a dream of what I thought "real" school was like, and ultimately what I would want for my kids when it came to their education.

I'd watch movies about high schools and the dramas between the cheerleaders and the football players and the nerds and the geeks. The snarky comments between kids as they went to their lockers. Lockers? Yes, please! There seemed nothing more glamorous to me than to have your very own locker, where you kept your "normal" textbooks (as opposed to my super Christianized

18

ones) and your Lisa Frank Trapper Keeper and bright pink lip gloss. I knew just what the interior of my fantasy locker would look like.

I'd have one of those full-length ones, the kind you could hang a full-length ball gown in (for prom, duh—because doesn't everyone hang a ball gown in their locker?), with several shelves at the ready. There would be a shelf for all my color-coordinated Trapper folders. There would be a shelf for my makeup and hair-spray. There would be a shelf for my cheerleading gear, because of course I'd be a cheerleader. I'd have a fuchsia-and-black framed locker mirror on the inside of the locker door, and I'd have super cute candids of my friends and me pinned to the door with heart magnets. I would line the back of my locker with contact paper in a cool black-and-white striped pattern, and *Seventeen* maga-zine would probably want to do a feature on it, something like "Top Lockers!" That article would reveal that I'd coordinated my locker at school with my incredible bedroom at home, a continu-ity of personal branding and sweet teen sophistication. My locker would always be super organized and cute and when that perfect guy stopped by between classes to flirt with me (as guys did in all the movies), he'd casually glance into my locker and be smitten and impressed by all that the condition of my locker implied— sweetness mixed with ambition, whimsy blended with smarts, a snapshot of a girl who has it all together and would be amazing to date. Clearly, my fantasy locker was the size of a small house, but I had a lot riding on this locker scenario.

In retrospect, it's startling to me that I had created such an image of what my life should be like based on the teen dramas and convenient rom-coms I'd watched so often. It set me up to think that life's script would follow a convenient path of boy-meets-girl, after which they face a series of comedic hurdles on their path to bliss, then everything wraps up neatly with a killer music montage and a romantic kiss.

In my real life, though, we were hustling from one small church to the next, staying as guests in people's homes—often people who were strangers to us—crowded into strange living rooms and kids' bedrooms on air mattresses. The only routine was a lack of one, save the familiarity of being on the road all day, making long hauls through the night to get to the next performance. So when I would wrap up my school for the day in the back of that Honda, eject that curriculum video from that travel TV/VHS unit, and push the next video cassette of a teen drama rom-com movie into the deck, I would gulp in the mirage of those stories and visuals and soundtracks with all the gusto of a traveler in a lonely desert.

In our spotlight-seeking culture, it probably sounds counterintuitive that I was fantasizing about a life out from under the lights. I loved singing and performing with my parents. I appreciated the attention, the fascination people had with a young kid who could sing, and, growing up in it, it was all I knew. I was grateful at the time and I'm still grateful today. But we humans, we always think there's something just a little better, don't we? We're always on the hunt for that thing that seems just beyond our reach, that green lawn on the other side of what has become our dusty familiar, and it makes us crave a swig of that idealized cup.

For me, nothing seemed more alluring than what I saw as all-American suburban typical.

A sip of "normal." A taste of "regular." A thirst for what I thought was better, consistent, enchanting, the glamour of a conventional childhood in a traditional home with customary parents holding down regular jobs so I could live the life I saw portrayed on those teen dream movies.

So it doesn't take a whole lot to figure out where one of my particular dreams came from. When Nic and I had our first son, Zealand, I stared in amazement at his tiny, beautiful face with his mesmerizing dark eyes and determined right then and there he would have a normal childhood. That was the dream. School—a traditional school right down the road from a real house with a backyard. A mom who baked cookies and served as homeroom mom and was at that school all the time, running the laminating machines to help his teachers. I'd give him a schedule and a routine. He'd have a desk at that school with his name Z E A L A N D printed on those dashed line strips, the paper then laminated and taped on top of his desk.

And eventually, ultimately, be still my heart, he'd have a locker. A locker where cute girls would stop by between classes and flirt. And, while his locker wouldn't be decorated like my fantasy femme locker, it would have a navy-blue mirror attached to the interior of the door, and it would have a bottle of aftershave on one of the shelves. His football gear would be stored in there for his after-school practices, and his books would be lined up in a masculine way. And those cute girls (because there would be many) stopping by would be so taken with his academic and athletic drive and would be so impressed with his personal tidiness, obvious maturity, and devilishly good looks. Of course, these weren't my only dreams for Zealand. There were others that carried far more weight and importance. But when there's something you feel like you've missed out on in your own childhood, you desperately want it for you own kid, silly or serious, locker or legacy.

What I thought were normal dreams for Zealand also felt exotic to me, or at least a level up from what I'd had growing up. I was convinced we would be Super Normal, a family living the suburban ideal. Yes, my level of romanticization of that ideal was consuming. Not to mention that what I was positioning as Super Normal was actually not the norm for a lot of people, just my projection from my Honda back-seat movie theater window on the world. But that projection was the target I longed for.

So I jumped in with both feet. We had our son Søren just fourteen and a half months after Zealand was born. We moved from our urban-cool condo in downtown Nashville to a standard cookie-cutter starter house out in the burbs, scraggly backyard and fence included. As the boys progressed through preschool, and elementary school loomed large, we upgraded to a house on a bigger lot that we could remodel and customize, in the school district we had heard rave reviews about. Zealand headed to kindergarten and Søren two years later. We established a solid school routine, and I began my career as Super Normal Homeroom Mom, laminating and errand running and copy making for teachers on a weekly basis, with many hours devoted to my children and their school experience.

We were making it happen. All the optics were right. To anyone who would care to take a snapshot of our daily family life, it was looking like, in the space of a film frame or two, I was achieving the dream I'd dreamed so many years ago in the back seat of that Honda. We were doing normal.

But a snapshot is different from the movie. And the behind-the-scenes film of our lives was a documentary, not a rom-com, and it was playing out very differently than the promotional pics.

Zealand as a baby was happy, sweet, smiling, and *so* easy. With a younger brother coming so fast on his heels, I had a built-in meter for evaluating developmental stages and phases. As the boys grew from babies to toddlers to preschoolers to kindergartners, it seemed as if Søren was lapping Zealand in some areas. I chalked it up to simple differences between kids. And, hey, Søren was getting the advantage of having an older brother to watch and copy, right? And Zealand had gifts in other areas, areas that weren't as obvious as Søren's more precocious, socially adept personality. So that would also play into it, right?

I reassured myself for a long time that those were the factors going on: their close birthdates and Søren's outgoing, social nature in contrast to Zealand's more thoughtful, serious one. And in my quest to be Super Normal Mom, I regularly took the boys to their wellness checks with my carefully selected and vetted pediatrician. He was the expert, and he wasn't saying anything about Zealand, so it all had to be good, right?

Right?

But in a plot twist that would have been movie-irony worthy, that normal, suburban, American public school, that thing I had sought so valiantly in the quest for a normal childhood for Zealand—it would be the very thing that would prove him unnormal, us as a family unnormal, and rewrite the script for all I had been seeking and dreaming toward.

• • •

We love to talk about dreams, don't we? Some of them we know are nothing more than a fanciful indulgence. At some point, we've probably all had to make peace with the fact that Zac Efron isn't going to show up with a dozen roses and serenade us in front of a stadium full of people. (And if Zac Efron has shown up with a dozen roses and serenaded you in front of a stadium full of people, you have to email me immediately because I NEED TO HEAR ABOUT THIS.) But overall, as a culture, and particularly in our faith communities, we often confuse what we call dreams with vision, goals, and God's calling.

A quick flip through a few social media memes and you'll always find it there—the compelling, cutesy sayings about you and your dreams and how it's all possible and how to make it happen. But a pithy, dreamy meme does not a reality make.

I've always been a big dreamer. I always have stories and songs and scenarios floating through my heart and my head. And you do too.

But being a big dreamer can sometimes bring crushing disappointment. And it's not because you didn't try. It's not because you didn't pray. It's not because you didn't put in the time and get up early and have the right connections and take advantage of every opportunity. It's because . . . life. Life happens. And it's also because, I think, we often don't really even understand our own dreams.

The good news? We're in good company.

• • •

He was the kid at the tail end of a big family. Not the oldest child with all the rights and responsibilities that come with that. Not the baby of the family with all the perks. He was next to last in a boisterous, messy family dynamic, and it could have made him a nondescript wallpaper in the family gallery, wallflower or not.

But he was a dreamer. A big dreamer. And he would proclaim what he'd seen in his heart's eye during the overnight hours to whomever would listen at the breakfast table the next morning, over bowls of whatever the ancient Hebrew version of Cheerios was.

His dreams involved imagery of sheaves of wheat bowing down to a sheaf that was his, seeming to make those brothers of his bow down to him—the older brothers who were forever

24

teasing him and bullying him and minimizing him. He told them of a dream where the sun and moon and eleven stars bowed down to him. That retelling even managed to get his father, Jacob, into an irritated dander. The kid may have just been trying to share the vivid and mysterious visions God was putting into his heart during the night, but his naivete about how the meaning of those dreams would be received by his older brothers and his father had far-reaching effects.

And the realization of his dreams would occur in a far different place under far different circumstances than he could have ever thought.

His name was Joseph, and all those brothers of his, the ones he was telling his achiever dreams to—those dreams in which God revealed Joseph as having a future that would put him as a man in authority—those older brothers weren't terribly impressed with his breakfast-table replays of his visions of position and power from the night before. To add insult to injury, they could see that their father, Jacob, loved Joseph just a skosh more than the rest of the kids, preferring to spend time with him, showing up with expensive gifts like a multicolored coat. So in their minds, it was no wonder Joseph was spouting off about how he was going to be the special one in his dreams. He was already living it as far as they were concerned.

Eventually Joseph's dreaming ticked off his dad too. Joseph told yet one more account of his dreamtime domination in the family line, and daddy Jacob chewed him out. Told him to check himself before he wrecked himself. (That's a Jaci interpretation of the original Hebrew. You're welcome.) And things were about to go even more sideways.

The brothers came up with an impulsive plan to get Joseph the heck out of Dodge. They sold him off to slave traders and conjured up a *CSI*-worthy crime scene, with an explanation that the wild animals must have gotten to Joseph while he was tending the family flocks out in the countryside. Their father, Jacob, bought the story, when all the while Joseph was being hustled far away to Egypt. And Joseph's reality those first few years in Egypt looked nothing like the nighttime visions that had danced in his head back home. Servitude. False accusation. Unjust imprisonment.

God had wildly and inexplicably interrupted the dream.

But it was while he was serving time for a crime he didn't commit that Joseph learned a new component of this dreaming thing. It was an important lesson in that season of interruption, one that he'd carry forward.

Dreams require interpretation. Sometimes that interpretation is something we want to hear. And sometimes it isn't.

Joseph encountered a couple of guys while he was serving time. They'd each had dreams and Joseph was able to interpret their dreams for them. For one guy, the interpretation was exactly what he'd been hoping for, a get-out-of-jail card. For the other guy, the interpretation was not what he wanted to hear: he was going to pay the ultimate price for his crime.

For Joseph, the season of interruption, even following these interpretations, lasted several more years until the Pharaoh himself had a dream that needed some interpretation. And finally, finally, someone remembered Joseph and the whole dream interpretation thing and brought him to Pharaoh's palace to decipher the dictator's dream. Joseph was careful to explain to Pharaoh that he, Joseph, didn't interpret—it was God who provided the interpretation. And after hearing Pharaoh's dreams, Joseph, through God's power, told Pharaoh what his sleeping stories meant.

That interpretation revealed news Pharaoh didn't want to

hear. But it also revealed a way through. It revealed God's warning and provision. And it ultimately all came true.

I wonder what Joseph was thinking all through that time. The dreams his fellow prisoners brought to him? They were fulfilled very quickly, within days. And those dreams Pharaoh had him interpret? Those dreams came with timelines and specifics, and it all happened. All this occurred years after Joseph's teenage dreams, and the others' dreams were fulfilled long before his own dreams were fulfilled. If I were Joseph, I'd be thinking, *What the heck, God? I can hear other people's dreams and figure out the backstories and what's coming next, but I don't at all understand my own dreams or, as the clock keeps ticking, how any of that is even possible at this point.*

But after God's interruption of Joseph's dreams, the interpretation showed up.

A famine hit Joseph's hometown, which was many miles and mountains away. His brothers stumbled their way to Egypt, where the rumor was that some super smart project manager for Pharaoh had been squirreling away wheat and provisions for just such an event. The brothers arrived, bowed, and begged for resources, not knowing that the guy they pleaded with was the brother they had mistreated so many years before. Ultimately, Joseph provided for the family, revealed who he was, reunited with his father, and moved the whole team to his locale.

It had been years in the making.

So. Back to those teen dreams of his. Did his brothers ultimately bow down to him? Yep. Did it happen quickly? Nope. And had any of them really understood the focus, the point of those dreams?

Absolutely nope. It wasn't about the bowing and the power play.

It was about God providing.

It wasn't about Joseph ruling over them and all the hurt feelings and outrage that ensued from his telling those dreams.

It was so God could feed them through the famine.

Oh.

Joseph had been a vehicle for interpreting dreams for others. And then God interpreted Joseph's.

It involved a far longer and more confusing interruption than Joseph ever could have imagined.

It culminated in an interpretation no one could have anticipated. And God's purpose in the repurposing of that dream was achieved.

• • •

Nic and I sat in a musty school conference room, backsides pressed into plastic seats, elbows braced on the faux finish wood table with a Kleenex box as the centerpiece, several education professionals seated across from us. We'd been called in for a meeting about Zealand, and my heart rate was at about the level of a jackrabbit being chased by a coyote.

The meeting I had been dreading was here.

I'd pursued answers to those little developmental hiccups of Zealand's, those moments in which he seemed to be just off step, like an audio track that doesn't quite match the action of the movie. I'd met with the pediatrician. I'd had the conversations with his kindergarten teacher and then the next year with the first-grade staff. We'd done some therapy for what had been called "pervasive developmental delay." There was a big scary word out there at the edge, unspoken but haunting me. I'd catch it out of the side of my heart's eye but blink rapidly away, willing it to stay out of focus.

It wasn't the first meeting like this we'd been in. We'd circled up during his kindergarten and first-grade years, everyone intent on helping Zealand with his developmental delays. But this was now the spring of his second-grade year and school was about to get harder. His grades were about to count more. And so the school wanted to meet with us again.

While I've been told I've got a giant personality, I'm not the tallest person. At all. As I sat in what felt like the most uncomfortable chair my rear had ever sat in, feet barely scraping the floor, I felt like a little girl hauled into the principal's office, about to get a stern lecture about what I'd been doing wrong, with a side list of further accusations and extra homework coming my way.

Nic sat silent by my side.

In previous meetings, there had been some big clinical words thrown around about Zealand and his challenges. A lot of them went over my head, and I would nod and smile, not wanting to seem dumb in front of the professionals. I mainly walked out of those earlier meetings feeling relieved that we had a plan in place to get Zealand back on track, to adjust a bit of his schooling to get him caught up to the other kids.

Not this day. This day, that ghost of a word, that phantom that I'd been able to keep clear of—it showed up. Sat right down in the middle of the table next to that Kleenex box. Leaned back on an elbow. Casually. Like it had been there all along.

Autism.

One of the teachers just threw it out there, a comment about Zealand's official diagnosis being autism, that he was on the spectrum.

And just like that, just as that terrifying phantom metamorphosed into something terrifyingly real, my dream crumbled and evaporated. All that I had dreamed of for me, for my child, that dream of Super Normal, in the presence of that one word, *autism*, was gone.

I left that meeting sobbing wildly. I bawled. I wailed. That word, *autism*, while it seemed to answer some questions for Zealand's teachers, only opened up a chasm of unknown chaos for me. What did all this mean? What did it mean for his future? What did this say about me as a mom? Nic stayed by my side, quiet and reserved. I rode a wild ride of emotion for days. I felt like I had lost any semblance of normal. I felt a warrior mom rising up in me, viciously protective of Zealand. I searched websites through tear-clouded eyes. Nic was supportive, listening to all my crying jags and questions and rages and sniffles. It wasn't until several days later, when I heard him crying quietly in the shower, that I realized the depth of the lost hopes and the complex grief that he was experiencing too.

We've come a long way since that raw meeting. We've learned a ton and have found our lives intersecting with amazing people who get us and get our son. Zealand is thriving and growing and making us laugh and keeping us fascinated by his unique approach to life. We've found peace amid the pieces of his diagnosis, and we've found some answers amid the many questions.

But what about my dream, *the* dream? Had I missed it completely?

Here's what I'm figuring out. And it's still a work in progress. My back-seat Honda dreams were a blend. A mixture of God leading and me inventing. That seed of a dream for Zealand, that deep desire I had for him to have a more predictable home life and a steady experience of school? It's exactly what is good for him. Being on the spectrum, he thrives best in that kind of environment. And it's also good for him that we do travel for our music careers. He's learned to be adaptable in those times we're on the road, and he thrives in the routine of being home. God has created the perfect blend for Zealand, from that compelling drive I had to provide stability and a school scenario that I didn't have, combined with the need to be flexible in those times we do need to be traveling for music. And I believe now that the compelling drive I had to provide this for him, that part of the dream I'd carried for so long, was absolutely from God.

But the rest of it? The popularity game and the fantasy prom and the in-crowd and the built-in soundtrack? Yeah. That stuff was all me. All the things I thought I was missing out on. Me.

And me is not Zealand.

So I'm letting God repurpose those parts of the dream. I'm letting him show me how he was directing me through certain elements to create what has been so very good for Zealand. The routine, the desire for stability, the continuity and predictability of a life anchored around traditional schooling, it fits Zealand and his needs so very, very well. I'm getting that interpretation now. And God's showing me how to let go of what I got all mixed up into that equation. I'm learning to dream new dreams. Dreams that have to do with the actual life he has given me, the actual people he's given me. I'm learning to listen for dreams that truly carry vision and promise from him.

Here's a verse that's helped me in this time: "'Let the prophet who has a dream recount the dream, but let the one who has my word speak it faithfully. For what has straw to do with grain?' declares the LORD" (Jer. 23:28). See, it's a beautiful thing for you and me to dream dreams and believe for supernatural or Super Normal, depending on your vibe. But that whole willingness to allow God to interrupt our timelines and that whole acceptance of his interpretation thing? As dreamers, we have to let his Word be the thing speaking most faithfully—not our expectation, not our interpretation.

Do I worry and fret about Zealand, about how people will interact with him? Absolutely. Are we still very much on the journey of raising a kid who is differently abled, with all the doubts and unknowns? Yep. Do I spend lots of time wondering whether he'll find love, a girl who will appreciate and embrace his unique nature? Of course.

But I don't pine anymore for the parts of those dreams that weren't God-given. And I'm seeing how God's interpretation of those dreams I had as a kid has far more to do with taking care of my son than it does with me fulfilling regrets or what I thought was missing from my childhood.

What dreams are keeping you from living your life now? Because, really, that's a nightmare. The prophet Isaiah, in Isaiah 29:8, wrote about how that feels: "As when a hungry person dreams of eating, but awakens hungry still; as when a thirsty person dreams of drinking, but awakens faint and thirsty still." To be so caught up in something that isn't your life—your true, singular gift of a life—to be trapped forever in a loop of comparison of your today against your fantasy, that's a torment. You may be standing in your nondescript kitchen, dreaming you were on a stage. I've stood on a stage, dreaming I was in a nondescript kitchen.

Okay. Not entirely nondescript. Wood floors, white marble countertops, all flowing into an open-concept living space. But still.

And sister, can I just tell you, any "dreams" we have that make us ungrateful before our God, any "dreams" that are allowed to spiral into disappointment with our today and dissatisfaction with our now, well, those are the kinds of "dreams" we need to do a self-check on. I've got to distinguish the difference between a God-given dream and my own agenda. It's not always easy to tell the difference. Some of my agendas can seem really good. But I'm learning that when I let what I see as unfulfilled dreams propel me toward ungrateful, unhelpful behaviors, then I can know I'm trying to do all the interpreting myself and I'm rejecting God's interruption and God's interpretation.

Maybe you're like me: when things aren't working out the way I envisioned, I'm charging toward food that isn't good for me, charging the card for that next pair of shoes I don't need, charging into emotions with my husband or those closest to me that can hurt and sting them. And that's when I can know that I'm hurtling away from a God dream and am letting a whole bunch of Jaci agenda take the wheel.

Hear me well. I'm not telling you not to reach for more. I'm not telling you not to take a risk in the direction of your faith. I'm all for it! What I am telling you is that there may be a lot of God in your dream . . . and there may be a whole lot of you that's snuck in there too. It's not that the blend is wrong: I believe that God often can lead us through the things we find fascinating and have a heart for, that elevate our purpose and mission on earth. I'm not saying that there should be no flavor of you in that thing you're pursuing. What I am saying is that God will often interrupt and interpret your dream in a way you hadn't thought of.

I do not like it when people interrupt me. I'm a fast talker, I've got plenty to say, and I need to get it all said. And I don't like it when things turn out differently than I planned. But God's gonna interrupt us from time to time. And he's gonna have a spin on our dreamy stories that we didn't see coming.

Now, you may get to experience that moment. That moment, down to the detail, that you've waited for. Maybe the lighting

God's gonna *interrupt us* from time to time. And he's gonna have a spin on our dreamy stories that we didn't see coming.

looks just like you pictured it. Or you weigh exactly what you thought you'd weigh. Or the people you wanted to be there will be there. The outcome will be everything you wanted. Awesome. Celebrate it. Thank God for it. But it doesn't mean that another dream in your life, one that isn't working out the way you would have preferred or planned, is invalid. It just may have a good dose of your agenda in the mix.

Embrace the interruption.

Listen for his interpretation.

And then begin to dream new dreams and allow him to repurpose the fulfillment of this one into a passion for the next.

Flip the Script

- That dream that's been in your heart, have you ever written it down? Take a moment to capture it. Not a list of goals to achieve. Not a pity list of what hasn't happened that you hoped would. Just that snapshot kind of a moment, what the realization of that dream would be.

- Now back up a moment from that snapshot you've captured. Ask God to show you what's truly at the core of it. Would the fulfillment of that dream bring you a sense of success? Worth? Belonging? Adoration? Completion? Healing? Is there an emotional need you're chasing in the guise of a dream? In my case, I was chasing a deep desire for what I saw as stability and fulfillment of what I thought I'd missed out on . . . and still ran into the uncertainty of Zealand's diagnosis and the worry that, even in a traditional school setting, Zealand would miss out on "normal." So what are you chasing? And if the dream were to turn out differently, can you be okay with that?

I'm really convicted by a verse from Jude. Some people think Jude was a brother of Jesus and other people say he was a cousin. Whoever he was in Jesus' family tree, I know these words of his really make me stop and examine my own heart when it comes to the things I'm pursuing and holding out there as "my best life." Jude warns people who are allowing their own understanding of their dreams to pull them away from living grateful, healthy, God-submitted lives. "On the strength of their dreams," Jude wrote, "these ungodly people pollute their own bodies, reject authority and heap abuse on celestial beings" (Jude v. 8). Is the pursuit of your dream leading to things that aren't healthy for you? Then could you be courageous enough to ask this question: *Is this a God dream or a Me dream?*

Three

Søren Smiles

Mom," he said, "when I grow up, I'm going to have a house with eight bedrooms. And it's going to have six beds for my twelve kids. And there will be a bedroom for me and Zealand. And it's going to have a bed for my wife and for his wife. And we're all going to live together."

That's what my baby, my Søren, told me.

He's just fourteen and a half months younger than his older brother. And let me tell you, having two babies just a little over a year apart? It does something to a girl's body. I remember trying to get down the aisle of a plane to get to a singing date when I was just several weeks away from having Søren. Even though I was still far enough away from having him that my doctor was in support of this trip and there was no reason for me not to fly, my, um, ahem, silhouette was a bit more dramatic than your usual gal in this stage of pregnancy. For someone who's always been considered petite, it was a reality check. My tummy and hips were banging into airline seats as I tried to maneuver down the aisle. People were looking at me with fascination and horror, as I'm sure they figured they would be witnessing a live birth in the air after the coffee and beverage service was over. My body weight almost doubled in that pregnancy with Søren. As big as I was, I knew he'd be a big baby.

What I didn't know was how big his heart would be. His heart for his older brother.

I'm the baby of my complicated family. I've got two older brothers from my mom's first marriage. I've got a brother and a couple of sisters from my dad's first marriage. I'm the only child of my parents' marriage to each other, so I have an interesting rung on the birth order ladder, baby *and* only, but not, in a modern family kind of way. My husband, Nic, is also the baby of his family, and since he's seven years younger than his older brother, he gets a bit of that whole "only child" dynamic too. His older brother seemed to live in a world Nic really didn't share when they were kids, given the age difference.

I know people who swear by the whole birth order thing, believing it has powerfully shaped their personality and motives. I know people who think it hasn't had that big an impact on them. What is true for me is that I loved being the baby sister, the baby girl. It made me feel special in a perplexing family dynamic. It gave me a sense of place in a huge extended family. (My dad is the middle child in a family of ten kids and my mom is the middle child of seven.) There were things about that role that I saw as part of myself.

When Søren came along, he was the baby of the family, the younger reflection of his older brother. I envisioned a day when Zealand would teach him guy stuff, when Zealand would take

Søren under his wing and teach him the ropes on getting math homework done, calling a cute girl from school, or learning how to shave. Big brother to little brother stuff. But those roles got far more complicated as the boys grew.

Søren started talking first, putting together more complex words and sentences. He interacted more. From an earlier age, he was easygoing and outgoing, engaging people with all the ease of a natural politician. His social skills contrasted with Zealand's more reserved approach to people and new situations.

Because the boys were so close in age, people understandably thought they were twins. People were always comparing them in size, height, and verbal skills. For a long season when they were both still little, in those toddler phases, we just thought Søren was ahead of the curve because he had the benefit of an older sibling. And a lot of that was true. He was always watching what Zealand was doing. But it was Søren hitting developmental milestones in contrast to Zealand's unique spin on hitting "typical" marks.

Maybe it's because Nic and I so relished our roles as the babies of our families of origin. Maybe it's because we both have described who we are by saying, "Well, I'm the baby of the family," as if that explains certain things about our personalities and approaches to life. Or maybe it's because Søren really is the baby of our family unit, the second cut on the parenting album after we got our parenting feet wet with Zealand.

We wanted Søren to be able to fully own that role as the baby. But God had a different role for him.

• • •

It sounded like a crazy idea. I had built my career through the radio—through recording music and then letting radio stations play my songs. Not *talking* on the radio about other people's music. And now these people were talking to me about being a radio disc jockey?

I was clear about my role as a singer. I understood where I fit into that equation, what was required, who I was in my role as a musician. But when I added the role of mom to musician, new responsibilities and desires popped up. No more late, late nights writing, recording, and generally living a night-owl creative's lifestyle. Remember, I had this deep need to provide stability and daily routines for my kids. So being constantly on the road and chasing lyrics until the wee hours, well, that was going to have to change.

I'd been making a few call-ins for our Christian music station in Nashville over the years. It was fun to interact with the morning show personalities, and I found that my interviews with stations across the country had given me a feel for how to chat it up on air, how to keep my thoughts within time segments. And I really loved keeping up on current trends and conversations, which also worked well when I was a guest on the show.

But I was still really surprised when the general manager for the station came to me with an idea I'd never considered. In a series of changes to the station, he asked if I would be interested in becoming part of a new morning team. It was called *The Family Friendly Morning Show* and it would go to more than one hundred stations across the country. I'd stepped in to guest host for a few months, but this was new territory, the idea of being a full-time radio host. It was a role that I hadn't sought and hadn't prepared for, but one for which God had been preparing me.

The boys were still in those baby and toddler phases, and I wanted to be home with them as much as possible as their primary caregiver, with as much consistency as I could, while still staying in the music and ministry arena.

Now, you may be thinking, how does being a radio personality on a successful morning show fit with that goal of creating a predictable home life? Fair question. But here's the deal: If you're getting up at four in the morning five days a week, lots of things in your life have to line up. At least if you want to be able to form complete sentences while you're on the air. And remember, this format of radio is live, so it's not like you can go back and edit whatever jumbled jargon you slung around due to a late night before. It's all out there in real time.

After praying about it I decided to take on this new role, and it meant a few changes. It meant that we had to create and stick to a strong routine to make sure I was getting good sleep before sliding behind the mic early in the morning. It meant that we could lean in to more steady financial planning since this role was a regular gig instead of the feast-and-famine of the music industry. For the first time in my life, I found myself waking up every day, commuting to the station around 4:00 a.m., prepping for the show, sitting behind the mic for four hours with my cohost Doug Griffin, wrapping up a few details, then heading back to the house, and arriving home just a little bit after the boys had finished breakfast. Routine. Five days a week.

The Family Friendly Morning Show would go on to be aired on more than one hundred radio stations across the country with 1.5 million listeners. It was a career role I had never imagined. Sure, there were learning curves and bedtimes that didn't get observed and days that went a little longer at the station. But for the most part, this new role I was living out met my family's needs in a way I couldn't have orchestrated on my own.

I did face some criticism from those who thought I was selling my music short. I was no longer able to take every singing date that came my way. The new job also changed how often I was able to record. I'm sure there were those who interpreted my new role as a relinquishment of my old one—as the girl with hits on the radio giving that up to become the girl talking about other people's records. It was a time of stretching, of letting go of certain ways I saw myself while adapting to a new persona: how other people saw me.

• • •

You've got roles you were born into. You've got your position in your family of birth. You've got the role your parents put on you, your role in the family dynamics—the dutiful daughter, the rebel, the comedian of the family, whatever that is for you. You've got the roles you've sought for yourself. Working girl, stay-at-home mom, volunteer, girlfriend, lover, friend. You've got the role you're known for in your community—the gal who's always positive or the one who can get the best stuff for the silent auction, or maybe you're the go-getter who's willing to volunteer for anything.

But as much as I have thought of any role as something permanent, something fixed by which I can define and understand myself, most roles have this little feature built into them: They change. They get repurposed. Sometimes we embrace the change or the different definition. Sometimes we don't.

Maybe you never pictured yourself in the role of single mom. Or stay-at-home mom. Or working mom. (Can we talk about that for a minute? *All* moms are working. Can I get an Amen?) Or single. Or single again. Or wife of an addict. And when that change in role comes, that place you never saw yourself in, what then? How do we understand ourselves in the wake of our roles not looking the way we thought they would? How do we square them up into the angles we thought made up the measure of us?

It's fascinating to read about the many people in God's Word who found themselves in roles they had never pictured themselves in. I'm pretty sure Noah, living landlocked in the middle of a continent, never saw himself as a master shipbuilder. Then there was Gideon, who was doing his best to live as a pacifist, and found himself at the front of a military unit, getting ready to take on Israel's most oppressive enemy. And what about Mary? Talk about a role reversal, from a virginal good girl to the gossipy topic of every kaffeeklatsch in the county, what with that whole teen pregnancy issue and all. And while we're on the topic of Mary, let's talk about her kid, Jesus. He was with God, he was God, standing outside of time and then *boom!*—squalling baby, potty-training toddler, synagogue-trolling twelve-year-old, oldest brother, perpetual single guy, controversial ex-carpenter, vilified social change advocate. And finally, receiver of capital punishment.

Yeah. Jesus gets the whole repurposing of roles thing, I'm going to guess. Paul reminded the early Christians at Philippi that being humble is the most important component of any role we are given. He reminded them that Jesus was willing to lay aside the glories he had in his identity as God and allow his role to become that of a slave.

The citizens of Philippi were generally wealthy. They lived in a small but important region. And the people Paul encountered there allowed their faith in Jesus to repurpose their roles in the community. Paul wrote in his letter to their church:

> Your attitude should be the kind that was shown us by Jesus
> Christ, who, though he was God, did not demand and cling to

his rights as God, but laid aside his mighty power and glory, taking the disguise of a slave and becoming like men. And he humbled himself even further, going so far as actually to die a criminal's death on a cross. (Phil. 2:5–8 TLB)

Lydia was a wealthy business woman who lived in Philippi. She had made a nice little business for herself selling purple fabric, which was a major fashion statement at the time, like our designer labels of today. People who could afford to wear purple clothing were seen as well-off, and they made Lydia well-off as her purple cloth became more and more in demand. She met Paul and Silas and was drawn to Paul's message about Jesus. Ultimately, she and all her household were baptized. Her home became a place of refuge for Paul and Silas after they were miraculously released from prison, and her home also became the place where the new church met in the area. A lot of historians think she helped financially support much of the mission work of Paul and Silas as a result of her belief in Jesus.

I have to think that she was inspired by Jesus' willingness to let God shape his role. Let's face it: it looks like she was living the good life in Philippi. A great product, a thriving business, happy clients. She could have kept coasting on that for a long time, without the hassle of having missionaries in her house, without the hassle of hosting church services, without the hassle of sharing her bank account. But God had other ideas. And now, all these centuries later, we read about Lydia, the fabric business magnate who allowed her role to be repurposed and became a major player in the spread of Christianity. All because she was willing to take on a new role.

• • •

That thing you were good at and that role you were comfortable in. That title you loved having in front of your name and the expectation you had that that role would continue forward, a definition of who you were. But then, things shift.

Sometimes it's because a spouse decides to walk out the door. Or the boss shows you the door. Or your aging parent needs you and you set aside that job you love to be there for them.

Or sometimes you've been trying to claim a role. You've put in the work. You've dreamed big. You've made the right connections, shown up early, stayed late. But that role isn't rolling out for you. And now you're having to face that perhaps that role wasn't meant for you. So now what?

Our roles are not static, even though we often think of them that way. We go from our parents' homes to our first apartments. We go from that intern position to manager. We go from being single to being someone's girlfriend to being someone's fiancée to being someone's wife. We go from being someone's favorite aunt to being someone's mama. When these expected roles shift in expected or gradual ways, we don't really feel the sting in their transition.

But when our roles get reversed, when the script gets flipped, when things are required of us that we didn't see coming and feel far outside of what we thought was our job description, it can feel unfair.

It's wanting things to be fair, for things to be predictable, that trips me up when it comes to this whole lane of being open to the role God has for me. For what he has for my boys. But I'm learning. I'm learning to smile with the roll of the roles. And part of how God is teaching me that, part of how he is showing me the rescript of my life, is through Søren's smiles. Søren smiles at the role he has, he smiles at his brother, and he smiles at his real life, his actual life, not saving a grin for some distant shore.

• • •

We were going to take only Søren on an upcoming spring tour. We were doing it to give him a break, to give him special attention. We were worried that he might be feeling the burden of his loyalty to Zealand. We worried that he wasn't getting to experience being the baby of the family. So we pulled together all the plans and had figured out a great solution for Zealand to stay in Nashville. We presented all this to Søren with a sort of "ta-da!" kind of jazz hands.

His response was not what we expected. His usual smile gave way to a quivering lip. And then his eyes welled with tears.

"I can't live a day without my brother!" he wailed.

Huh?

We tried to explain that this would be a time we could focus on just him, that it could be a special time just for him and his daddy and me. But Søren wasn't having it. At all.

So we ended up taking both boys in a very crowded Sprinter filled to the gills with our band and team because Søren couldn't go a day without his brother. Honestly, Zealand probably would have been just as happy staying home with the spoiling grandparents—he actually might have been happier, given that he could have stayed on his preferred routine. But Søren wouldn't have been as happy without Zealand.

Søren's is the voice that drifts out. It drifts out in advocacy, in inclusion for his brother. With Zealand along to experience life on the road, Søren smiles.

Were we paying attention, not wanting Søren to feel over-burdened or overly responsible? Of course. But here's one of the mysteries and beauties of wearing your repurposed role well: it makes a more complete you.

In the wake of the dramatic diagnosis of autism for Zealand, it could've been easy to miss. Yes, Søren is protective and amazing with his big brother. But I was reminded recently that Zealand also invests in his relationship with his little brother. And it makes Søren more complete.

I was recently flipping back through some old videos of the boys on my phone. I smiled at the birthday cake candle-blowing archives, found myself stunned at how much taller they are than some footage from just a few months ago. I kept scrolling back and went to those videos that just open up all kinds of mama feels, those little fragments from when they were toddlers.

Mamas, take videos. Keep them. Upload them to lots of places. Trust me on this.

And there it was, this clip. Søren at about nineteen months old, smiling a grin as big as Christmas. Zealand, two and a half years old, stomping around in front of his baby brother and then jumping at him, pretending to scare him. In this little glimpse of the past, Søren giggles and cackles at each attempt of Zealand's. And as he laughs, he says over and over in his squeaky little toddler voice, "Happy! Happy!"

Søren isn't really all that interested in what the typical role of the baby of the family is. He's living and is happy in the tailored role of the baby of *this* family. And in *this* family, that makes him the baby brother of big brother Zealand. And God is customizing that role just for him and equipping him for it.

Søren laughs.

Søren cares.

Søren advocates.

Søren protects.

Søren dreams.

Søren smiles.

• • •

What is a role?

I did a little deep dive into that word *role*, wanting to understand where it comes from. Turns out it's something cool. Really cool. The word *role* comes from the word *roll*. Not like a crescent roll, though I am a fan of those. *Roll* like how they used to carry parchment or paper, a writing surface that was rolled up. It's how they used to carry important documents, scripts, and papers of identification. A roll would be the script for an actor, the document that would give the actor his lines. It's the same word you find in the word *scroll*, that written material that is rolled up.[2]

One of my favorite verses in the Bible, Psalm 139:16, says, "Your eyes saw my unformed body; all the days ordained for me were written in your book before one of them came to be." Be sure and check out *book*. In the original Hebrew it means "scroll."

Whatever role God has you in, he provides the roll you need: the words, the wisdom, the inspiration. Even when you don't feel prepared for the role. Even when the role doesn't seem to fit. I started to find more and more verses that showed me the connection of *role* and *roll*. This verse kept jumping out at me: "I will give you the words I want you to say. I will cover you with my hands and protect you. I made the heavens and the earth" (Isa. 51:16 NCV). In other words (pun intended), God will provide the words for our scripts.

In Scripture, Solomon didn't feel ready for the role he received. Technically, he wasn't the one who should have received the throne after the passing of his father, King David. He wasn't the oldest son whom the crown usually went to. He wasn't even the second or the third or the fourth son. He had plenty of older siblings who were in line to take over the kingdom. And yet he found himself in the role of king. He told God,

> I am a little child; I do not know how to go out or come in. And Your servant is in the midst of Your people whom You have chosen, a great people, too numerous to be numbered or counted. Therefore give to Your servant an understanding heart to judge Your people, that I may discern between good and evil. For who is able to judge this great people of Yours? (1 Kings 3:7–9 NKJV)

In response to Solomon's humble request, God gave him the *roll* to lead, the words and the script that led him to be considered the wisest king. God repurposed Solomon's position from one of nineteen sons of King David into the son who would carry his father's legacy as king.

Jesus also repurposed the roles of his disciples. He took a bunch of guys who had never had debate training and never been to Bible college. And he gave those guys the leading roles in the early church. He made them pioneers, this diverse group of people from various areas of the Holy Land, who had been leading different lives, some as commercial fishermen, one as a tax collector. And because they'd been following Jesus, it wasn't long before they found themselves in all kinds of situations they never could have imagined. Jesus encouraged them and reminded them that he would provide the roll for the role:

> You will be brought before governors and kings for My sake, as a testimony to them and to the Gentiles. But when they deliver

. . .

Whatever role God has you in, *he provides* the roll you need: the words, the wisdom, the inspiration.

. . .

49

you up, do not worry about how or what you should speak. For it will be given to you in that hour what you should speak; for it is not you who speak, but the Spirit of your Father who speaks in you. (Matt. 10:18–20 NKJV)

• • •

It's funny that I would have such an idealism about my role as the baby of the family. Whereas most people consider the baby of the family to be the role that gets all the spoiling and all the extra attention, because of God's plan, I became the breadwinner in the family. I became the one who was financially providing for my extended family for a period of time, as they put their lives on hold to help me with my recording and travel schedules through my teen years. It was a role reversal, to become the caregiver to those who had been my caregivers. So it should be no surprise that God would not be confined yet again in my life by giving Søren a "typical" role.

I was up at the boys' school recently, right before the start of the school year. I was helping get some things ready. I was determined to be that Super Homeroom Mom, cape fluttering in the wind. I'd brought the boys with me, and they were at a table in the cafeteria within my line of sight, chatting quietly with each other, waiting for me to finish. One of their teachers, Mrs. Green, walked through the cafeteria and saw them there. "Boys, I need some helpers," she told them. "Could you help me put some books out in my classroom?" She caught my eye, tilting her head for permission, and I nodded back. The boys popped up, ready to take a break from all the sitting. They trailed after Mrs. Green, ready to show off their volunteer skills as the Sons of Super Homeroom Mom.

After a while, Mrs. Green returned to the cafeteria with them, mission accomplished. They took their seats back at the table while

Mrs. Green headed my way. She approached me with a wistful smile. "I've got to tell you about the boys, Jaci," she said.

"Were they a problem?" I asked.

"Not at all," she said. "Let me tell you what happened. I asked the boys to set books out on some tables at the back of my classroom, displaying them nicely so that my students would be sure to see them on the first day of school. I began placing stacks on the tables, and Zealand jumped right in, spreading them out across the tables. But then Søren followed behind and reorganized the books. He set them like I had described, artistically displaying them so that the pop-up books were opened to show the artwork inside, standing some books up, and straightening along the way. When we were finished, Søren motioned me aside and whispered, 'Mrs. Green, sorry about that, about the books. I haven't taught him how to do that yet.'"

Mrs. Green and I held gazes for a long moment, then looked back over at the boys, who were sitting back at the cafeteria table. We looked back at each other, and Mrs. Green's eyes filled with understanding and kindness.

I haven't taught him how to do that yet. It was the first time Søren had most clearly identified his role in Zealand's life, the role that exists and is more important than his birth order in the family. The role he was truly born to take on and equipped by God to carry out: the protective, compassionate guide of a baby brother.

May we all learn to roll with the role.

Flip the Script

- What is a role you feel you were assigned in your family of origin?

- What is a role you "inherited"? That place where you had to step into the gap, fill the spot on the bench, even if it was a position that you didn't think fit you or didn't align with your personal goals? What did you learn from that inheritance?

- Is there a role you've been hesitating to take on? Is it that manager position at work, the one that seems scary because of the responsibility that goes with it, and you struggle to see yourself in the role? Sometimes I've had a script running through my head that tells me I'm not educated enough, not experienced enough, not wise enough to take on a role that seems out of my reach. But so often I've come to realize that's just been the Enemy trying to keep me down. What step could you take today, this week, to explore taking an additional step toward a role you're a little scared of?

- Is letting go of a role you've cherished hard for you, like needing to retire as Super Homeroom Mom because you've packed the last kid off to college and it's time for a new generation of homeroom moms to make their run? If you're in a season of transitioning away from a beloved season in your mom life, your work life, whatever that is for you, take some time to think through not what you feel like you are losing but what could be on the horizon. It's so easy for us to get stuck in a time of transition and only look back at what was. What could be on your horizon? What interest have you had on the back burner for a while? What vision do you have of yourself, of who you want to be, in this new season of your life? What steps can you take today to begin walking toward that future?

Four

The Blur

I wasn't born a diva.

No, to become the kind of diva I became takes a lot of time and work. It was a project years in the making. And, ultimately, it would take my full endorsement and participation.

I was born in Houston, Texas, the youngest and only child my parents had together in their complicated marriage that included my half siblings and step siblings. The way my mom tells it, from the beginning she felt that I would have fame in my life. My name is actually a nod to that sense of hers: she intentionally wanted my name to be J-A-C-I, four letters, easy to sign autographs with, like C-H-E-R.

My mom has some big vision. Bless her.

She began entering me in pageants while I was still in diapers. They tell me I won Prettiest Baby in Texas while I was rocking my Pampers, then Cutest Toddler a couple of years after that.

You would have thought I would have been a shoo-in for the next pageant my mom entered me in when I was seven. It's actually one of my first memories, being in that pageant. I got to wear a white dress with a crimson-red sash. I sang Whitney Houston's "Greatest Love of All," because if you're gonna go diva, you might as well go big.

But, alas, I came in second. Second place. My parents had decided they wouldn't let me wear makeup in that pageant, and it gave all those other mascara-and-lipstick-wearing seven-year-olds the cosmetic edge, I guess. And they all did big hair, I mean BIG HAIR, with the curls and swirls and glitter hair spray. And they all had sequins on their dresses and mine was just plain white. Maybe if I'd been all glitzed up, I could have taken first. Maybe.

Getting second place wasn't what I, or my parents, had planned. It wasn't part of the script. And part of why I think that pageant is one of my earliest memories is because its echo has long been a driving motivation in my life.

That echo? Rejection stinks. Avoid rejection at all costs.

Rejection bounced around in my heart. It whispered in my head. It told me that if I could have been just a little *more*, a little brighter, a little better, a little more glittery, then maybe, just maybe, I could have had that first place in people's hearts, on the judges' scorecards.

Now I don't think my mom ever intended to introduce rejection to me through those pageants. It was supposed to be fun and a way to experience performing and dressing up and meeting other little girls and their moms. But I remembered its sting. Its message. Its cold shoulder turned in my direction.

It wasn't too long after this experience that our family went through a significant shift. My dad had been a pastor in Houston, but when I was in third grade, we moved to Denton, Texas, near

Dallas, for a ministry position. My dad has openly talked about what a desperately challenging season he faced in that time in Denton. He entered a deep depression, one that almost cost him his life. He still gives sermons about sitting in his car, with a voice in his head telling him to end it all, to drive his car off the road and finish off the pain. And he tells about experiencing God interrupting that moment and hearing, *David, I have a ministry for you.*

In the end, my dad grabbed hold of the hope of God having plans for him: that he had something further to contribute in this life. We moved away from Denton and went to Tomball, Texas, where he became the worship pastor for a church. And it was then that we began heading out on the road more and more, to bring music and hope to churches near and far.

It was summertime when we headed out for our first longer music gig road trip. I was nine years old and had finished up my fourth-grade year. I didn't think too much about it, being on the road. School was out, my friends were all heading out with their families on vacation, and I was headed out with mine, albeit with a little different purpose. When I think back to those first few extended weeks on the road, practicing singing harmony parts as we drove along major highways and obscure back roads, I thought it was all an adventure. I was simply with my parents and following their lead, both in how our summer was unfolding and in my harmonies to their melodies.

But when fall came around, we were still on the road. Still traveling place to place. I never went back to my little elementary school in Tomball, Texas, and the back seat of that Honda became my new classroom as the singing dates just kept coming. I got a lot of attention for being so young and having such a comfortable presence on the stage. Among our little trio, my mom, my dad, and me, things started to shift, and I was getting featured more and more. Little by little, I was starting to take the lead vocally. But I was closely managed by my parents.

I certainly felt the pressure and expectations of the churches we were singing for. This was our family business, this road show. It was important that we make the people at these places happy. It was important that our reputation was good with them. Performance for me didn't just mean singing; it also meant being a good girl, kind, sweet, full of Scripture and faith. It all came from a real place. And there was a real pressure there, a clarity of the importance of what I was living and projecting.

Three years later, I slammed into rejection once again. Yep, at the age of twelve I thought my career was over. Twelve. Twelve?! What twelve-year-old is even thinking (a) they have a career and (b) that they have enough of a career that it could be over? Um, this twelve-year-old, that's who. I had gotten it into my head that I needed to become part of a group called the Continental Singers. They were a group of young vocalists with a long tradition of performing. Each year there would be auditions to add new vocalists to the group, and I just knew this was the next step for me. We headed for Estes Park, Colorado, for the Seminar in the Rockies where I would be part of a pageant-type experience. I would move from judging panel to judging panel at the large encampment where the seminar was held, singing and harmonizing, in the hopes that I would become one of the newest members of the Continental Singers.

I faced the judges for the first round.

And then I was cut. Done. Finito.

Rejected.

After receiving the news, I ran back to the motor home we were living and traveling in, threw open the door, and hurled myself onto the thin mattress of the queen-size bed at the back of the chassis. "It's over!" I wailed to my parents, tears soaking my face. "My career is over!" And I really did think it was. "I'll be living in this motor home for the rest of my life!"

Bonus points for dramatic flair when faced with failure.

But it was real. It was intense. I was getting kudos in the churches as the cute young kid hustling from town to town with my parents, singing and talking up the gospel when other kids my age were passing notes in class and flirting with boys. But when I was evaluated and judged alongside a passel of other cute, young, intense, gospel-toting kids in that audition for the Continental Singers, I came up short. And it made me question if I measured up at all.

• • •

That fear of being judged, of not measuring up, can impact the script of our lives in significant ways. For some of us, a rejection means that we stop trying. For some of us, a rejection makes us try all the harder. For all of us, rejection comes in with a great big red pen and scribbles some really mean and nasty stuff all across the careful life lines we had been crafting for ourselves about the purpose and meaning of our lives.

When a fear of rejection is well-fed through our thoughts, through the practice of focusing on it, it creates a vulnerability, an exposure that makes us more and more susceptible to the bite of rejection. For some people, it seems to make them disconnect from others. They try to avoid rejection by spewing rejection at anyone who comes around them. You see this kind of strategy at play with that infamous mean old lady down the street, the one who yells at the kids for riding their scooters on the sidewalk in front of her house at two o'clock in the afternoon, as if this were some kind of delinquent behavior. You see it in the boss who seems aloof and disengaged. You see it in members of your faith community who come in a little late to church and leave a little early, seeming not to want to be bothered with developing relationships. Sometimes at the core of all that is someone who simply doesn't want to get rejected again, so they do the work for you by not allowing you to get close.

And then there is this other kind of response to rejection's exposure, the one I see now that I trafficked in for years. That response is to try to protect yourself from rejection by doing all you can to please those around you, to become what you think they expect you to be, to attempt to follow the script they're giving you to read from.

. . .

That fear of being judged, of not measuring up, can *impact the script* of our lives in significant ways.

. . .

Now, understand, sometimes what you think others expect of you is actually not even what they're thinking. Sometimes we can build a whole persona based on what we believe people want of us, whether it's true or not. And sometimes people really do have expectations. They really will extend or withhold the love, the acceptance, the approval we crave as rejection refugees.

That was the case for me: I was a blend of deeply loving God, loving to minister to others about his love through music and ministry, with deep currents of wanting to please everyone I possibly could. Out of my love for God, I truly wanted to live for him. From my earliest days, I've always felt his presence, his joy, his creative Spirit coursing through my veins. I accepted him as my Lord early in my life and never looked back. I wanted to live according to his Word. I wanted to show my gratitude by making godly, wise choices in my personal disciplines and behavior.

That has never changed.

But what was also hard for me was that ironic drive to avoid rejection. To, yes, please God, but also to please people. And that combination would gallop and nip at my heels as my career caught gear and my mom's early vision of fame for my life took shape.

• • •

At twelve, following the rejection by the Continental Singers' judges, I thought my singing career was over. By thirteen, I'd been "discovered." Through a series of connections, I'd been asked to sing for the National Week of Prayer event in Houston. Someone who heard me there then got in touch with my parents and asked me to open for a Point of Grace concert. A road manager video-taped that performance and it was sent to two women who were looking for a new album project—Debbie Atkins at Word Publishing and Judith Cotton Volz of Myrrh Records. Debbie and Judith flew out to see me perform in Houston at an event my parents had booked for me specifically so Debbie and Judith could hear me sing. I opened for a band at that event, singing to tracks, which is when a singer performs not with other live musicians but to a prerecorded set of music. Following me was the featured group, and of course, they had a full, amazing band. I gave it my all, and Debbie and Judith were kind.

Then Debbie and Judith headed back to Nashville, and I was left to worry that I had looked second-rate compared with that full band, that I must have seemed pretty low bar with my little prerecorded tracks and only myself on stage. We didn't hear anything for a while.

Until three plane tickets to Nashville showed up and the record label flew us to Nashville to talk about next steps. I was signed to a record contract with Myrrh Records, part of Word Entertainment. I had just turned fourteen. And we officially moved to Nashville to begin work on the album.

At that point, I'd been living on the road for almost five years. To suddenly have a home base in Nashville was surreal. We moved into an apartment with two bedrooms, and I had my own bathroom. My own bedroom. Heck, my own bedroom door.

That first recording contract wasn't some huge financial windfall. There was a small budget for producing the album with the requirement that we would have one year to finish it. A small check was cut to me. While I was extremely excited and grateful to have been signed, the actual money details of the contract were very modest, and my expectations were even more modest. I didn't really think much would come of the record and was hoping it would just recoup the production budget and that little check that I had received.

We got to work. My mom would drop me off at the studio and I'd get my headphones on and get in front the microphone. I'd recorded before; I'd made "custom" records with my mom and dad, which is an album you make independent of a recording contract or major studio. We sold those on the road as we traveled, me hauling cassette tapes and CDs to the folding tables in the church lobbies where we sang. But recording in Nashville, with the powerful machine of a record label behind me, was a new experience altogether. Even though I was just fourteen and turned fifteen during the production of the album, I was treated with a lot of respect and deference. People listened to what I said.

They listened to my ideas. At the same time, I didn't assert myself all that much. I was very aware that this was all sort of an experiment, a gamble on the part of the record label. I listened as well, to the musicians and producers. I was beyond grateful for the opportunity and I was ambitious to do my best. I understood that our reason for moving to Nashville was attached to how well I performed on that album.

Day in and day out, my mom and I continued our unique car pool drop-off, me packing up what I needed to take with me for the day, bypassing the schools near our apartment, yielding to school crossing lanes and laden school buses picking up kids. We'd roll up to the studio and I'd grab my backpack and head in for a different kind of education—the studio my classroom, the production team my professors, the microphone my mascot.

I was happy. My parents were happy. The managers and producers were happy.

And everybody was about to get a whole lot happier.

My first album, *Heavenly Place*, released in 1996. I had just turned sixteen. The first single was "If This World," and it became a number one hit. Then the next single from the album, "Un Lugar Celestial," was released. And it went number one. So did the next one, "Flower in the Rain." And as 1996 clicked over into 1997, "On My Knees" and "We Can Make a Difference" were both released as singles. And both went number one. All those number one hits meant that *Heavenly Place* went platinum, which means it sold over a million copies.

Here's the math: a debut album from a relatively unknown artist that goes platinum equals all kinds of happy, happy people, from the artist to her parents to her record label. It was an incredible experience. And I was thrilled to know that people were being ministered to by the songs on that record. We would receive letters and messages from people from all walks of life, telling us how certain songs, certain phrases on the album, were helping to reconnect them to God, that they were exploring their faith again, that they were discovering connection to a Father who loved them.

The magnitude of that kind of meteoric jump was just beginning to dawn on me. There was a brief moment, like that slow pause right before a wave hits the shore. You feel it coming, but for a beat, it's quiet. And then the wave hits and everything moves, even the sand under your feet. And when that wave of the meaning of all this hit me, when the accolades and the pursuing by record execs and all the rest started to surge in, the roar, the tumult was huge.

· · ·

I have compassion for King Saul in the Old Testament. I really do. I mean, I get that he became a villain in the life of David, the best friend of his son Jonathan, the one whose music could calm Saul's vicious headaches, the one to whom God would ultimately award the kingship of Israel. I get that Saul was all kinds of awful to David and that Saul made all kinds of awful decisions, including walking away from God.

But I also see something in his life that I understand. Saul became dependent on trying to please the people of his nation. He didn't want them to reject him in favor of David. He struggled to be patient when God told him to wait for certain things. He became impulsive and tried to fix things he thought were going wrong.

On one occasion, the prophet Samuel told Saul to go wait for him at Gilgal for seven days. Saul was to wait with his army, a band of men who were supposed to be loyal to Saul. Samuel assured Saul that he would be along in a week. But the Philistine army was in the region and Saul and his men started to get scared. The days passed and Samuel hadn't shown up yet.

And then the thing that Saul feared most began to happen: his men began to scatter.

Saul decided he had to do something to keep the men from rejecting him, from leaving him. So he took it upon himself to do something that was beyond what God had told him to do through the prophet Samuel. He decided to make a sacrifice. He took it upon himself to change the very specific script of God's command.

Now, that doesn't sound like such a big deal, does it? It seems like, to me, on practically every other page of the Old Testament, somebody was firing up the barbecue grill and roasting something before God: sacrifices for sin, sacrifices for gratitude, sacrifices as payment. It was part of life before Jesus came as the ultimate sacrifice for our sins, ending the need for this kind of practice.

But when Samuel arrived and realized what Saul had done, he was quick to tell him what a mistake it was.

What? Why?

It's in 1 Samuel 13 that we find the answer. When Samuel arrived at Gilgal and discovered what Saul had done, Saul tried to explain it all: "When I saw that the men were scattering, and that you did not come at the set time, and that the Philistines were assembling at Mikmash, I thought, 'Now the Philistines will come down against me at Gilgal, and I have not sought the Lord's favor.' So I felt compelled to offer the burnt offering" (vv. 11–12).

Did you catch it? Saul sacrificed, but not out of reverence or obedience to God. Saul acted out of fear, out of his worry about the men scattering. About people leaving him. About his popularity and reputation as king suffering. And so he got out ahead of what he was instructed to do. He got nervous and impatient. He tried to preempt what he saw as a coming rejection.

And it didn't go well. Samuel strongly chastised him, telling him that he would ultimately be replaced by someone who would follow God's heart. But just three chapters later in the book of 1 Samuel, it's clear that Saul still hadn't gotten the message. This time, he was given very specific instructions about how to conduct an attack against one of the enemy nations to Israel, the Amalekites. Again, Saul hedged the bet. He acted out of his own wisdom, allowing the men of his army to take plunder that God had instructed them to destroy. Saul was still buying friendships, still trying to carry insurance against rejection.

When Samuel called him on the carpet again for what he had done, listen to what Saul said: "I have sinned. *But please honor me before the elders of my people and before Israel*" (1 Sam. 15:30, emphasis mine). Saul was still so focused on avoiding the rejection of the people. He loved God. He was trying to do right. But rejection had become his governing idol. And in seeking to avoid rejection, he ended up rejecting the God who had offered him everything: a nation, a kingdom, and a legacy.

I have to ask myself, *How often have I been governed by a fear of rejection? How often have I attempted to make what looked like sacrifices to God that were ultimately an attempt to keep my people from scattering?*

And what about you?

I've made plenty of bad decisions in an attempt to keep my people from scattering from me. And I'll bet there's plenty of stuff you've done, too, from putting *up* with poor behavior from some of the people in your life in an attempt to hang on to them, to perhaps putting *out* some poor behavior to push away those you were afraid might ultimately reject you. Avoiding rejection can be a wildly powerful motivator, and I'm still learning the ways it has propelled me through the years. But be encouraged: when we start to call it out in our lives, when we start to understand how it hamstrings us and tangles us up, we can begin the process of emptying it of some of its power.

•   •   •

I have a very good memory. My friends often comment on my recall for names, for events, for dates, for conversations. I didn't realize how strong my memories are until I began the process of writing this book and was surprised by my ability to put myself back in time, to look around, take in the sights, hear the sounds, recall the feelings. But when it comes to the months following the release of *Heavenly Place* and then the release of my second album, *Jaci Velasquez*, well, it gets foggy. I call it The Blur. So much started happening so fast.

There are moments that stand out. In 1997, I was invited to the Dove Awards, the Christian music industry's annual event that recognizes outstanding achievement in the faith music lane. I remember shopping for an outfit, so excited to have been invited. I remember the gal named Robin who did my makeup. It was all so far from how I had gotten ready for the gigs I'd grown up with, my mom and me crammed into a small gas station bathroom, trying to make some kind of style of our hair and smooth wrinkles from our road-weary outfits before we headed into the next small church to sing. New outfits and makeup artists? What was this? I arrived at the Dove Awards thankful and dazzled and dazed by the lights and the big names.

That was the night I won New Artist of the Year. If I thought life had been moving fast over the previous couple of years, it was just about to get supersonic.

I was contracted to do a Target commercial. Yes, that Target— the place I love to spend so much time now. And it was while I was on the shoot that my manager came to me with a new contract for a new album. The label wanted to re-sign me. And this new contract would be in my name; I was turning eighteen. My parents wouldn't be on this contract. And it was for so much more money than I'd ever thought was possible. I would be able to buy us a house. A whole house.

I signed.

Then Sony Discs signed me to do a Latin album. It led to the opportunity to do a crossover album in Spanish with Rudy Perez on Sony in 1998. The first release on that album hit the top of the Latin charts, and something opened up that I'd never seen coming: an offer to do a Latin pop album. That album also had a song that went number one, and I had two different songs, in two different music markets, that were ranked by Billboard as number one hits at the same time.

And then more advertising contracts started coming in, from a number of big-name products. With those contracts came a huge shift in how people treated me. I'd experienced people's kindness before. I had appreciated their compliments and affirming words. But now, there was a completely new dynamic. Anything I said went.

It sounds strange, but it was true. As the singles on my second record, the *Jaci Velasquez* album, went number one over and over, and then as the Latin albums started to roll out and the Grammy nominations for those albums started to roll in, people began to tiptoe around me. They began to jump as I spoke. Water bottles would appear in my hand before I asked. Gifts would appear from notable people in the industry. People around me would scurry and hustle when I made the simplest request. It seemed like everyone was clambering to keep me from blowing up, as if my temperament were some kind of volatile and unpredictable thing. That wasn't me at all. I was a girl who loved God, who knew the value of living according to the fruits of the Spirit. But all around me were people who wanted to satisfy my every whim. Ultimately, I learned the power of a pout to get what I wanted when I wanted it. I learned the efficiency of a temper tantrum to end a creative or managerial debate. It seemed like everyone expected me to behave and react like a diva. And so I did. And I paid for it.

I don't just mean on down the line, in spiritual and psychological ways. I mean I literally paid for it. I'd go out to a restaurant with a group of people . . . and I would pay for everyone's meal. It was expected. We'd head to a movie, and the tab was on me. I also had an increasing number of friends and family on my payroll, some with really important roles and definable duties, some a little vaguer. They knew I was paying; I knew I was paying. It all made for perfect conditions to grow a diva.

To be clear, I take full responsibility for my transition to diva during this time. I truly did have a pure heart about serving God, and I truly did maintain many of my core values during The Blur. So even though I was boy crazy, with my pick of guys who loved to be around the glitz and the fame, it was important to me to be a virgin on my wedding night, and I did wait for marriage. Even though I knew that my paying for everything was putting a disproportionate power *and* responsibility on me, I was at heart a generous person and felt strongly (and still feel strongly) that generosity is important to God. But mixed into all of that good intent was a girl who could snap her fingers and have people stand to attention, ready to head out on whatever errand I deemed necessary.

Ironically, in the middle of this season, with as much of what I see now as embarrassingly spoiled brat kind of behavior, I was also still being heavily managed. With the success of the albums came a heavy tour schedule. I found myself back out on the road, not in that old blue Honda, not in that creaking motor home, but in a luxury tour bus with all the gidgets and gadgets. I'd sing at a packed venue one night, sign the autographs, do the meet and greet, and head back to the bus, finally drifting off to sleep in the predawn, the miles rolling beneath the bus wheels rocking me to sleep. I'd be up again early, a list of call-in radio interviews commanding my morning. I'd get a quick break for lunch and then we'd arrive at the next venue and do a sound check. I'd head back to the bus for another round of drive-time radio and magazine and print interviews followed by a fast dinner, and then it would be time to get ready to head out on stage—hair, makeup, and outfit in place. I'd take the stage, perform, pray with people, hear their stories, sign the autographs, head to the bus, and do it all over again. Practically every minute of every day was accounted for and scheduled and owned.

Somewhere in all that coddling and controlling, I was losing my true sense of myself. More than ever, there was so much riding now on keeping rejection at bay. There were so many people now dependent on me fulfilling what was expected of me. They needed me to be the biggest personality in the room, with the clearest demands. They also needed me to be the darling of the Christian faith industry, a golden child with a squeaky-clean reputation. It deeply impacted my relationship with my parents. I was now literally the boss, with them working for me. I was a daughter, but an employer daughter, a very strange CEO position for someone at my age. I was a friend, but an employer friend, a dynamic that doesn't often yield the kind of friendships that are based on complete honesty and equality. During The Blur, everyone wanted me, wanted something from me, wanted to be seen by me. I felt like I was watching a film in which I was the movie star, but it didn't seem real. It was like it was happening to someone else.

And I was still running from rejection.

I would never want you to get the impression that I had some sense of "Oh, poor me!" Never. I was so crazy thankful that I was getting these opportunities, and it was dizzying to try to get through all the doors that were opening so fast. But that's part of what's funny about things lining up for you, when you're getting to do things and meet famous people and go to amazing places that you never thought you would. You can get scared. Scared that it's all going to go away. Scared that it could end. Scared that you won't get picked for the next album or the next commercial or the next awards show.

And so the roar of possible rejection gets louder, sometimes equally as loud as the joyful noise of gratitude.

As a means of staving off that fear, I suppose, I always had a boyfriend in my life, always the next boyfriend lined up. I craved the validation of a romantic interest. But if I felt the least flicker of waning attention from a guy, if I felt the slightest cooling, I would break up with him. Immediately. And install the next version of boyfriend in his place. And I had a weird habit where as soon as I broke up with a guy, I'd change my phone number immediately. I can't even remember how many numbers I went through. I told myself at the time that I didn't want any of my old boyfriends bugging me.

Now I know better.

Really, I didn't want to know if he never contacted me again. I

didn't want to know if he didn't find it worth pining over me, trying to call, leaving me desperate voicemails. I didn't want to know
if he walked away without a second thought. In changing my
number after a breakup, I was protecting myself from knowing
if he never reached out again. I wasn't worried he would contact
me again; I was worried he wouldn't.

As my career kept gaining altitude, my parents' marriage
came crashing down. I was nineteen when they told me they were
divorcing. It was a twist of the script that I didn't see coming.
Our trio was breaking up. They had moved out of the house I had
bought us, and I was now traveling on my own more and more,
tour buses yielding to first-class flights and first-class flights yielding to private jets. But their divorce brought not only the reality
that they were ending their relationship but also the feeling that I
was somehow being rejected, as if somehow I hadn't done enough
or hadn't tried hard enough. I said in an interview following their
divorce, "It was horrible. I secluded myself from everybody and
everything, and was angry with God. I prayed, 'How could you
let this happen?' I was sure it was my fault."[3]

I was extolled as an "overnight success," but from the time
I went on the road with my parents as a nine-year-old until the
release of *Heavenly Place* at the age of sixteen, I had spent half
my life pursuing this music thing, ministering to people through
music to introduce them to the God I loved. And once I finally
saw things coming to fruition in my career that I could have never
dreamed, it was only three short years before my parents' marriage came apart. In the middle of this meteoric rise in music was
the crashing comet of constancy. It was the simultaneous launch
of myself into adulthood and the loss of how I thought I fit into
my parents' relationship. I was now in the biggest pageant of my
life, with record companies and radio stations and advertisers

making high-dollar decisions every day as to who would get picked and who wouldn't. For a girl who had been running from the possibility of rejection for most of her life, I was now running straight toward it, with everything riding on me staying squarely in the expectations that had gotten me to this place. And in this place, the ground seemed to be made up of equal parts quicksand and crevasses.

Flip the Script

- When was the first time you remember feeling rejection? Was it not getting an invitation to the cool girl's slumber party that all the other girls in your class were invited to? Was it something you tried out for that you really wanted to do but didn't get picked for, like cheerleading or marching band? What kind of impact do you think that had on you moving forward? Did it make you more tenacious? Or more timid to take risks?

- What are some things you've put up with in relationships as a result of fearing rejection? Was there an unhealthy friendship you maintained for far too long? Was it a romantic relationship? Or what about a job situation that you knew was not a great fit, but you stayed because you were afraid of "future rejection," worried that you wouldn't be accepted by a new employer if you left your current position? What was the cost of staying in those unhealthy situations?

- If you could begin to remove a fear of rejection from your life, what would change for you? What dream would you chase if you could make peace with the fact that you might not be able to achieve it?

- How important has it been for you to be "picked" in your life? Have you craved the validation of being "chosen" by someone? I want to encourage you to decide that to be chosen by God is enough. And put this verse somewhere that you can see it often: "For we know, brothers and sisters loved by God, that he has chosen you" (1 Thess. 1:4).

- Here's a fascinating little thing about rejection that I've learned: it *sometimes* masquerades as competitiveness. We try to avoid being rejected by being competitive, by trying to beat others, by trying to always win, because if we win, well then, we're winners. How competitive are you with others? And here's a fascinating little thing I've learned about competitiveness: it *often* masquerades as jealousy. Do you sometimes struggle with feeling jealous of the achievements and lives and relationships of others? Could a feeling of rejection be lurking at the bottom of it? How might your perspective on winning and jealousy change if you could identify the strains of a fear of rejection that might be lurking there?

Five

Sour Lemons

I accidentally got married.

And I intentionally got divorced a little more than twelve months later.

I can try to explain it by saying that I was scrambling to control my critics. That I desperately wanted to be a "good girl" in the eyes of others. That I waited until that first wedding night for sex. I can say that all the events leading up to that accidental marriage and intentional divorce were supposed to make things better, were supposed to make lemonade out of sour lemons.

It began with a whim that I didn't think would actually go anywhere. It all started with an audition.

It was a first toe-dip into exploring the whole acting thing. When I went to the audition my manager had set up, it was merely a chance for me to learn about the audition process, what it was like to stand in front of casting directors and run a few lines. It would give me a little insight into the industry so I could use it at some point down the line, after I had some acting chops and experience under my belt. I'd been a huge movie fan my whole life, and it seemed like such a fun thing to do, to get to go on an actual movie audition, sort of a little bucket list kind of a moment.

And then the unexpected happened: I got the part of Patricia, a spoiled, prim-and-proper debutante from New York City, in the film *Chasing Papi*.

Well, that escalated quickly.

My manager and I had an emergency huddle to figure out what to do. The movie was going to be a romantic comedy telling the story of a guy juggling romances with three different women in three different cities. Step one: we would need to set some boundaries on what I would and would not be willing to do on set, realizing that the director might decide to retract the offer after I put in my "good girl list." I wouldn't cuss. I wouldn't kiss anybody, not even the handsome male lead. I wouldn't wear anything too revealing, no matter what my female costars might wear. I'd stayed true to my faith so far, developed a clean reputation in the Christian and Latin music scenes, and I didn't want that to change.

Step two: I would need to move out to Beverly Hills to be on set for the next several months. We'd need to find a place for me to live that would be close to the movie lot. I'd be living on my own for the first time in my life, away from my parents and away from the Bible Belt towns, Houston and Nashville, in which I'd been born and had lived.

Step three: I needed to get my parents and boyfriend to sign off on the whole caper. I figured they would be cool with it, but I wanted to make sure.

My manager and I sort of assumed that step one would shut

everything down. Directors don't like to be told what their actors will and will not do—especially by a girl who's never been in a movie before, is a relative unknown in the Hollywood scene, and is saying she won't do a list of things that were pretty minimal in the movie world. I steeled myself to lose the part based on my good girl requirements.

To our surprise, the director agreed to my list. *Okay then.*

Step two moved along smoothly. I found a place to live in Los Angeles and moved in, ready for life on my own. After a few months I even had a roommate. She came from a similar faith background as mine and her parents had been in full-time ministry too. She was trying to make her way into the Hollywood spotlight in music and film, and our agents thought we would be a good fit. Her name was Katheryn Hudson, one of the most charming people I've ever met. We became fast friends in that isolated time, but ultimately our lives started to head in different directions. Today, you'd know her as Katy Perry. Yep. That Katy Perry. So, living situation figured out.

Step three, getting the seal of approval from my parents and boyfriend. I thought this, too, was in the bag.

Not so fast, dude.

My mom was not a fan of this idea. At all. She had lots of concerns. I chalked up some of her worry to the idea of me moving out on my own, and I tried to reassure her I was ready for stretching my wings. She remained negative about the whole deal, particularly the movie. I finally stopped trying to convince her and wrote her off as a controlling mom who was going to have to come to grips with letting her little girl go.

And then there was my boyfriend, Nic.

Nic Gonzales. Handsome, talented, devoted, kind. We'd met while on tour together. He was the lead singer for Salvador, a

Christian band based out of Austin, Texas. We'd flirted for a while, which then led to hanging out after performances. Then it led to a dinner date and then another one. After a while, we took that step of DTR, "defining the relationship," becoming boyfriend and girlfriend. Surely Nic, my encouraging, visionary, accomplished Nic, would be all for this film opportunity.

Um, that would be a no.

He was not happy about it. Couldn't square this opportunity with where I said I wanted to go with my music. Hated the idea of me moving to California. Questioned my motives in wanting the role. We fought. Fought some more. He told me again and again that he thought this was a bad idea, that he didn't see how it could lead to anything good. I reassured, yelled, comforted, snarled.

Then came the day that something just clicked in me. Clicked, as in, clicked off. I was done. Done with all of Nic's objections. Done with him trying to hold me back. Done with him trying to control me. *Sour lemons,* I thought. *Nic's just jealous of this jump in my career.* Sour lemons. *He's totally worried I'll find someone else.* Sour lemons. *He should trust me.*

So I decided I didn't need my mom and boyfriend to sign off wholeheartedly on the movie. I just dulled the concerns and objections of my mom and my boyfriend to whispers in the bigger stereo sound of opportunity and movie dreams. I wasn't blowing them off, but I wasn't asking for their permission either.

There. Step three taken care of. I dusted my hands off, the gritty sand of my mom's and Nic's objections slapped from my palms, leaving me freshly ready to grab the wheel of my life. I accepted the role and headed to the movie lot.

I credit all those years of riding in the back seat of the blue Honda with preparing me for being in front of a movie camera. All those miles that I watched movie after movie on that boxy

TV/VHS combo unit, I guess I really was paying attention. Not just to the layout of the stories and the special effects, but how the actors "told" those stories through their expressions, the delivery of their lines, and the subtleties of their interactions and reactions. Being on set, in front of the director and cinematographer, felt natural to me, and I ate it up. I developed friendships with my costars Sofía Vergara and Roselyn Sánchez, who played the roles of Cici and Lorena, my two "competitors" for heartthrob Thomas's true love. Director Linda Mendoza was easy to work with and made my first experience of movie making fun.

And, to some degree, I was playing a role that I'd been playing for a couple of years at that point. My character, Patricia, was a coddled New York City socialite, a diva complete with a fluffy dog under one arm and expensive designer bag slung over the other. In some ways, that had become the character people expected of me in my "real" life, that of a celebrated Christian pop star. They would jump at my slightest question, hustle to fulfill any request, and act like I might just go off on them at any moment. In my heart of hearts, that was never who I was, but because of how young I was and how big my career had gotten, it became a reality to a degree, which meant I could immerse myself in the role pretty easily.

The shooting of the movie took several months. While I was happy with the work, I was also trying to navigate new friendships in an unfamiliar city. I'd be on location from early in the morning until late at night. On those rare occasions when I'd have a little time off, I was in a completely new world: the Los Angeles social scene. It was exciting, it was alarming, and it was completely different than anything I'd experienced before. I'd hang out with my roommate and some people in the music and movie scenes.

As the movie was nearing an end, I made another big change

in my life. Nic had just become too outspoken in his objections about the Hollywood life I was leading, and I had grown tired of it. He would regularly ask what I was doing and who I was hanging out with. I had been feeling suffocated and confined by his input and his opinions. The long-distance relationship we'd been conducting, him in Austin, me in Los Angeles, wasn't easy, and I wasn't feeling a need to go back to my "old" life. There were exciting new horizons out there, and I sometimes felt like Nic was trying to pull me backward. He was the person in my life who would call me out and stand up to me, and I didn't like it anymore. Didn't he understand who I was becoming? It all came to a head when I stayed out until the wee hours one night at a party and didn't pick up any of his frantic phone calls trying to locate me.

Soon after, he came to town to visit me. We sat on a park bench overlooking the Pacific Ocean and talked. Then I broke his heart. I broke up with him. I thought, *If he can't get on board with my newest dreams, my freshest open doors, then "see ya."* In my shortsightedness, I told myself I needed only people around me who believed in me, who wanted every slice of the cake for me. Couldn't he see that? I felt so right, so justified.

By the time the movie wrapped, I was living in a strange tri-fold kind of world. I had started out in contemporary Christian music, then added Spanish Christian albums to the mix, then Latin pop. Up to that point, I'd been able to keep all three of those worlds happy. But all that was about to change.

Each of those music markets had expectations of me, and when *Chasing Papi* was released in 2003, I realized for the first time just how different those expectations were.

The Latin pop market felt like my role in the movie was consistent with how they saw me, a squeaky-clean kid who was singing some great dance music and romantic ballads for them. They were supportive, thought the movie was fun, and celebrated with me.

The English-language Christian market and Spanish-language Christian market weren't so dazzled. Christian movie review sites were highly critical of my involvement in the film. Fans of my music openly questioned my morals and choices. Respected Christian leaders advised parents to keep their tweens and teens far away from the film. It hit such a fevered pitch that I felt like I had to respond. I wrote an open letter on my website:

> I hear that there are many questions about the movie, especially now since people are seeing the trailer or previews out in theaters. To put your minds at rest, no, I haven't left my personal faith in God, and I don't ever intend to. . . . I am grateful for the production company, because they allowed me to change and edit several scenes that I was uncomfortable doing because of my beliefs. The process of deciding to enter Hollywood was a very thoughtful, prayerful one. I constantly consulted my family and pastor to make sure I was answering my calling.[4]

It was all an unfamiliar, bewildering territory. I'd long been a golden child in the eyes of my Christian world. And now I was muddied. I was going to do whatever it took to polish my reputation back up to sparkling. I was going to figure out a way to make the sour lemons of criticism into lemonade.

• • •

I think highly of Moses' brother Aaron. He tried to make lemons into lemonade. He liked the reputation he had as the priest of the Israelites. He enjoyed people looking up to him as a role model.

But that all started getting questioned when Moses went up that mysterious mountain called Sinai to have a conference with God. When Moses had been gone for forty days, the Israelites started to get restless. In Exodus 32, they demanded that Aaron make some kind of god that they could see, something familiar and more like the Egyptian life they had just escaped from.

So Aaron, in an attempt to make lemonade out of their sour lemons, stirred up a concoction of melted gold from their jewelry. He cast the melted gold and crafted it into a golden calf, his effort at returning to the status as a golden child among the people and quieting the critics. He created an altar for it and announced there would be a big festival the next day. He threw in that it would be a party for God . . . with an idol in attendance.

Seems to me that's what a lot of us do when criticism comes our way. We try to fix it our way but say it's for God. I know that's what I did.

Moses came back down the mountain and realized what was going on: a big, wild idol party. He was beyond livid and tore down that golden, fake lemonade calf. He ground it into powder, mixed it with water, and made the people drink it, a bitter cocktail of idolatry and human effort.

Making that movie was one thing. What I did next was a golden calf move, nothing short of an Aaron kind of attempt to take the sour out of the lemons. But instead of making a golden calf, I was attempting to cast myself back into my golden child reputation. I tried to salvage what I felt had been damaged by the release of *Chasing Papi*. I'd been dating a new guy for a little while, and it was getting more serious. I truly thought I was in love, really believed that I could make a marriage with him work, and craved the idea that this would put to rest the negativity and embarrassment from the blowback of the movie.

It was a whirlwind romance with a fellow musician, someone I'd known for a handful of months before we started planning a wedding.

I can look back at the timetable now and shake my head in wonder at what I was doing. That's why I say I "accidentally" got married. The scramble to try to "fix" what I thought I'd broken in making the movie made for poorly considered choices. *Chasing Papi* came out, the criticism started coming in, and I married this guy within about three months. I look back on that wedding day and I remember feeling shocked that I was in a white dress and the music was starting. I remember walking down the aisle thinking, *This is a huge mistake.* But I thought I was so far in at that point, so far into worshiping an idol of damage control, that to be a runaway bride would have only messed up my golden child reputation further. So I continued my trip down that aisle.

It didn't take long for the wheels to come off that brand-new marriage. We were two very different people, with different goals and visions for our lives. We were both traveling constantly, separately, for different tours and recording dates. We had moved into the big house I'd purchased in Nashville, and I once arrived home from the road to discover that my new groom's entire band was living in our home. We had no time for privacy or building a life together before I'd head back on the road again. I basically never unpacked. I lived out of my suitcase, whether in the house I owned or in a hotel room. Eventually, that new groom would find new affections and I wouldn't fight to try to keep the marriage together. I called the game, filed, and fled. Which brought down a whole new bushel basket of sour lemons.

• • •

There's this festival in the Old Testament that I relate to. It's called the Feast of Tabernacles, or Sukkot. It's still celebrated today in Jewish communities and in some Christian ones as well. It was originally laid out in Scripture to be a seven-day experience, usually in the early fall. People would move out of their homes into tents for that week. It was to be a reminder of the forty-year period when the Israelites were living in the wilderness in tents as God was bringing them to the promised land, and his faithfulness when he brought them into their new homeland and into having cities and homes to live in.

One part of the Sukkot celebration in particular stands out to me. The people were commanded to gather the fruit or branches of specific trees in the region and to bring them before God:

> On the first day you shall take the fruit of majestic trees, branches of palm trees, boughs of leafy trees, and willows of the brook; and you shall rejoice before the LORD your God for seven days. (Lev. 23:40 NRSV)

The "fruit of majestic trees" was understood to be the fruit of a particular tree in the Holy Land. It's a fruit called an *etrog*. Its textured rind has a bright yellow color. It's a kind of citrus, so it has some sour bite to it. It's—wait for it—a type of lemon. The people would wave the etrog before God, along with three other types of plants or branches, each day of Sukkot. That waving of that etrog, the Holy Land version of the lemon, was to signify that God is the God of the harvest. He is the one who provides a sense of home and blesses and makes life sweet.

In that season of my life when I was on the road constantly, never unpacking my suitcases, I felt like I was wandering around, desperately trying to figure out where to land. And I was collecting etrogs, lemons along the way, but instead of raising them up to God, I was trying to make what was sour sweet. I was using all my own ideas and strategies. But raising something up before God, waving it before him, means turning it over to him.

Do you feel like you're camping out, not really living in the center purpose of your life? Do you feel like you've been making the same circle through the same set of circumstances but it never gets better? Have you been trying to "fix" things, scrambling to make up for one mistake that led to another, then another, then another? I speak from experience: it makes life sour.

It might just be time to unpack. It might just be time to grab that suitcase of sour you've been lugging around. It might just be time to spread it all out before God, confess that you've been trying to fix it all, and let him sort it out.

> Raising something up before God, *waving it before him,* means turning it over to him.

*   *   *

Did I accept that movie role because I was chasing a bigger career, one that might include acting and moving into a wider spotlight? Absolutely. Did I ignore the advice of my mom and my boyfriend at the time, Nic? Yep. Did I throw myself fully into a hasty marriage and inevitable divorce that led to my record company dropping me? Yes ma'am. That would be me. Absolute lemons of mistakes.

But God made some lemonade out of all that sour.

I can tell you that one of the other actors in the film sharply teased and barely tolerated me the whole shoot because of the good girl list I required of the director. I can tell you how that same person, years later, became a believer in Jesus and contacted me to apologize.

I can tell you how all the fallout from the movie's reception, and my attempt to fix it, ultimately led me back to Nic Gonzales, that guy whose heart I had broken because he dared to be honest with me about his concerns. I can tell you we wouldn't have the love story we now have, had we not walked through what we did.

I can tell you that all those events caused a huge reset in my life and a renewed passion for sharing God's goodness through music and through film.

But I worry. Worry that you'll hear it as justification.

Here's what I do know. However it all turned out, I didn't go into the decision about making the movie with my heart in the right place. I fought back against my mom and boyfriend being so opposed; I assumed they were operating from a place of selfish motives, when I was the one steeped in self-interest. They wanted what was best for me, but I marched onto the movie lot that first day with a couple little chips of rebellion and "I'll show them" sparkling like bling on my shoulders. We like to listen only to the people around us who tell us what we want to hear, only those who "believe" in our dreams. But sometimes the people who love us best might just love us enough to bring some sour to the table. And we're wise to listen.

Here's the weird part about how the equation sometimes works. We'll often reject opinions from those closest to us. And we'll embrace and try to fix and doctor the opinions of those who are watching us from afar, those people chiming in on social media or from "company headquarters." That's certainly what I have done in my life.

I thought God's answer had been yes to the movie; I got the role, after all. It didn't really occur to me that it might not have been his yes but rather a yes from the Enemy. It's just possible that God's answer was coming to me through the people and family who loved me best and knew me best and could foresee how this film was going to be received in the Christian community. And, let's not forget, the Christian community is *my* community, my brothers and sisters in Christ. I know we get all worried about judging each other and having our noses in each other's business too much. Jesus even warns us about making sure we're paying attention to the log in our own eye rather than being focused on the speck in our brother's eye. But when we are operating at our best, we are supposed to be there for each other. We should speak into each other's lives and offer wisdom and warning and counsel. And God can speak through that.

A friend recently asked me if I really, *really* thought making the movie was a mistake. After all, so much good, so much sweet lemonade in my life ultimately came out on the other side of that decision. I'd beaten myself up about it for so long that I had to stop and think.

At the end of the day, I still don't know how to answer her question. There was so much of my own ego and drive and impulsivity, and goodwill and ill will, wrapped up in the whole thing.

But here's what I do know: once I stepped out of the tent of a messy life I was living in and turned all those sour lemons over to God, he repurposed the whole thing.

Whatever the state of my heart when I stepped in front of that camera. Whatever others thought of the storyline of the movie and if a Christian had any business taking part in it. Whatever you think of my poor matrimonial patch job. Whatever the fallout from those decisions, whether someone thinks it was deserved or not. Whatever failure or frailty I brought to the whole thing. God repurposed it all in ways I couldn't have DIYed.

Here's my question to you. What are you trying to fix in your life? What things aren't lining up the way you planned, making you feel that drive to do something, anything, to change the opinions of others around you?

Now, I'm an action kind of person. I don't believe in sitting around and hoping things will change. I charge in, start taking names, troubleshoot, and get in motion. That's a good thing. I've known a lot of people who don't ever put in an effort to try to make changes in their lives when things aren't working. Is there a time to be still and wait on God? Absolutely. But there are many, many times when God tells his people to get up, dust themselves off, and get busy.

So I'm not talking about *not* setting things into motion. I'm talking about the *means* by which we try to fix things. You've got things in your life, opportunities and messes, some sweet, some sour, that you're needing to make forward progress on. But before you start diving in, before you begin your own attempt at making sour sweet, here are some things to ask yourself.

Flip the Script

I've got to admit, this chapter was a tough one for me. It's hard for me to look back on this season of my life. I feel like I'm reliving the mistakes, reliving the shame that I felt. That girl making those decisions, making those mistakes, she's not the person I know myself to be. And yet there she is. Maybe you've got some things in your life that are the same way for you. Hard to look at. Harder to talk about. And yet, when we can have the courage to bring those things out into the light, it can be an encouragement, a warning, a transparent wisdom for someone else. So I want to ask you to be brave. I want you to wisely tell the part of your story that doesn't match the script for how you wish you would have acted, for the decision you wish you would have made. And answer these questions: Who can benefit from the mistakes and decisions in your life? What do you wish someone would have shared with you about "lemons" they made? And how can you courageously and transparently use your story to help others?

- Why do you feel the need to quiet your critics? This was a big one for me. If I'd felt so certain of my decisions in that season, I might not have been so intense about trying to get people to calm down. In retrospect, I can see that I had my own concerns about my path. I wanted all kinds of freedom to make these decisions, but I didn't want to pay the price that some of them would require, which meant including some people who disagreed. When you're really solid on a decision, when it's really something God has confirmed, quieting the critics won't matter to you. I look at Jesus' example when he took the unexpected route of being arrested, then put on trial. Back in the Garden of Gethsemane, he had resolved that he would walk onto God's path. He was so sure about it that he didn't put up a defense, didn't back down, and didn't scramble to justify himself. "But Jesus made no reply, not even to a single charge—to the great amazement of the governor" (Matt. 27:14).
- How far are you willing to go to try to gain approval? So, obviously, I was willing to go pretty far to try to repair things with people who were disappointed in me. Which led to a whole series of further issues. What have you been willing to do? Go into debt to try to buy people's validation, trying to carry the right purse, drive the right car, live in

the right neighborhood? Hang out with the wrong crowd? Dive in to a big gossip session with your fellow mom gang because they are the ones who control the PTA?

• This is one of the verses I need to return to over and over. I should probably just go ahead and print it up in a cool, modern font on white paper and put it in a modern black frame (of course): "Am I now trying to win the approval of human beings, or of God? Or am I trying to please people? If I were still trying to please people, I would not be a servant of Christ" (Gal. 1:10). I think this verse can keep us out of so much trouble when it comes to attempting poor patch jobs. If we mess things up, a healthy dose of repentance and getting right before God is far sweeter than covering one mistake with another, then another.

Six

Resetting the Clock

I went to London, England, to learn Spanish. That was my official reason, at least. And I really did learn a bunch more Spanish while I was there and went to class and studied.

But I also went to hide. My intentional divorce was underway. My attempted DIY fix for the whole good-Christian-girl-makes-a-Hollywood-movie bit had now left an impact crater in my reputation that was far, far beyond anything I could repair. I'd already been on shaky ground with my record company during the process of the movie, which had only gotten worse after the blowback when the movie was released. And now, in the wake of good-Christian-girl-makes-a-Hollywood-movie, marries-a-guy, divorces-a-guy patch job, they, ahem, declined to take me on for another album at the end of my current contract, which is a very nice way to explain that they fired me. Basically.

I get it. I really do. They had invested in a girl in her teens with a sparkling reputation, who was embraced as a role model by parents for their daughters. And I'd been that for them for many years. I thought I was that. I thought all that effort and achievement was me. But I had confused my reputation with my character. And when it all blew up, I attempted repair job after repair job until the spackle and the paint couldn't hold up the wall anymore.

So I went to London. Because obviously that's what you do when you think you've destroyed your career in another country. You pull up the tent stakes and set up camp somewhere else, not really factoring in that you're taking with you the one thing that started the whole mess: you.

I'd been in London a few times before and loved it. When I was seventeen, I did a European tour that was simply amazing. My band and I spent a lot of time in Germany, the Netherlands, and England on that tour, and the crowds were incredible.

I also spent time in London when I had the opportunity to work with Martin Terefe, a legendary composer and producer. He had worked with Coldplay, Jason Mraz, and so many other incredible musicians. The time I spent with him working on my album *Beauty Has Grace* was one of the most remarkable of my creative life. That album was an edgier, more raw sound for me, and I got to truly explore more of my artistic depths. I grew as an artist during those weeks spent at Kensaltown Studios and caught some vision for where I might be able to head as a writer and vocalist.

While recording the album, I stayed at the Hempel Hotel, which was this super cool hotel right by Hyde Park. The interiors were right up my alley: long white lobbies with expansive white sectionals and crisp black accents. Guest rooms with clean, spare walls, simple beds, and deep bathtubs. All very minimalist, clean, intentional, and so very chic. I'd come in from a full day of creative collaboration and swirling ideas and giddy fatigue and arrive at this serene, calming oasis, the perfect complement to the previous feverish hours of music creation. I can absolutely point to the Hempel as a huge source of inspiration for my home decor style today. That album, that collaboration with Martin, and that stay at the Hempel were seeds for understanding more of who God had created me to be, instead of how I'd been crafted by the people around me for years.

Two years later, when everything came crashing down in the States, with my reputation tattered and my recording contract running through the shredder, I felt this pull to go back to London, where possibility and growth had felt so close. Plus, nobody knew me there. I could escape all the explaining I was having to do in the States.

So I sold that big old crash pad of a house in Nashville. Sold all my stuff, all that cool furniture. Bought a plane ticket. And bolted.

Check this out. When I say I bolted, I'm not kidding. I got on FindaFlatmate.com (or at least I think that's what it was called), an online place to connect with other people looking to share living space in expensive cities in Europe. Or possibly a great way to have a movie like *Taken* written about your experience. I went for it anyway, cyber dangers be hanged. And that was how I found my hilarious, free-spirited Scottish roommate. We shared a flat in Notting Hill. Yep. That Notting Hill, of the Hugh Grant–Julia Roberts movie fame. Because, remember, I have this movie obsession thing. So I was in a Notting Hill flat (Why is the word *flat* so much more charming and sophisticated than *apartment* or *loft*?) with a virtual stranger I had met virtually. If one of my boys tells me he is going to jump on a plane and find a roommate on the internet, I'll have a heart attack. To my mom's credit, though, she kept all her objections to a minimum. This decision would either be the most courageous or the stupidest thing I'd ever done.

Was I scared to go? Absolutely. But I was more scared to stay. Scared I'd make more mistakes in the reach of the public eye. Scared I'd try another fix-it idea that would make things worse. Scared I'd run into people who knew my ex-husband and I'd have to try to explain it all again. Scared I'd fail further in front of people.

I took my failure risk private and trusted FindaFlatmate.

It was terrifying, and it was liberating.

I was alone. Not lonely, but alone.

I hadn't known there was a difference between the two, but I was learning. Since my teens I'd always had a boyfriend. Many of those boyfriend relationships were puppy-love, teen-crush kinds of encounters, but I had lived in a constant cycle of being pursued, being caught, being lovesick, being enchanted, being disenchanted, being heartbroken, back to being pursued, over and over. I took a huge part of my identity from where I was in the given cycle at any moment. Boyfriend to boyfriend, relationship to relationship. And it wasn't just the constant romance thing. I'd been chaperoned, coddled, managed, scheduled, appeased, prodded, spoiled, placated, and manipulated from the moment I stepped onstage for the first time. That had only accelerated as the records sold and the contracts got bigger and more and more people depended on me for their jobs and paychecks.

A typical day at the height of my career at that time was a full-on dawn-to-dark endeavor. While on the road touring, I'd be woken up early to jump on radio interviews to help promote upcoming dates on the tour. After a few rounds of interviews, I'd get a short break, get some school work done, then be back at it, giving phone interviews to magazines and newspapers. During this time, we'd be driving to the next venue, setting up, and then it would be time for rehearsals and sound check. We'd get those completed, I'd gobble a quick meal, then it was in to hair and makeup, and then time to hit the stage. I'd wind up the show, do meet and greets with the folks, decompress after performing, hit the hotel bed or the tour bus bunk, and then start all over again in the morning. I didn't know such a thing as private time or being by myself. My whole world was in the presence of other people, whether that was with those closest to me or those who would drive miles and buy tickets to be close to me.

Not so in London, licking my wounds, where my Scottish flatmate was hilarious, fun . . . and couldn't have cared less who my stateside persona was. She hadn't heard of me and, frankly, didn't care. She hadn't signed up to be my bestie; we were aligned simply to make London real estate more affordable for each of us. She was involved with a guy and had a job and had her own set of friends. We got along just fine, but she didn't need me to fill any gap in her life, short of making sure my part of the rent was in on time and I took out the trash on my assigned days. Those first few months in London, I didn't really know anyone. I ate by myself, grocery shopped by myself, took the tube by myself, studied by myself.

Studied, because, remember, I had come to London to escape, yes, but also to learn Spanish. That's a perfectly normal thing, right? To go to the motherland of English to learn Spanish? But there really was a great Spanish school there, and I wanted to expand my fluency in Spanish. I wasn't raised in a home that spoke Spanish, even though my family has a Spanish last name. When I was first approached about recording a language cross-over album when I was eighteen, I jumped in with both feet to quickly learn conversational Spanish. To my surprise, I was able to pick up elements of the language with relative ease. When I would be interviewed by Spanish reporters and media personalities, they were so kind with me as I searched and fumbled for the right words. Everyone had been very gracious. But at this point in my sagging career, it seemed that Latin pop might be the one lane left open to me—the audience that hadn't judged my appearance in the movie and didn't care too much about my messed-up first marriage. So I wanted to make sure to give myself the best chance at that, to be able to communicate and read and joke and write with higher proficiency in Spanish. So I went to class. Studied. Learned.

And I learned not just better Spanish-speaking skills, but how to be alone. Especially how to be alone with God.

My relationship with God had also been a public one. The adoration people would hear in my voice when I sang, the expressiveness I used onstage to communicate the lyrics, the interviews I gave about my choice to remain a virgin until marriage to honor God, all those things were sincere, but they were also seen and heard and read about by many other people. Now, in London, away from those more public experiences, I had time to hang out with God in a way that was completely new. Yes, I was a mess, and I was searching and failing and scrambling and flailing, but it was all between God and me now—no comments on websites, no radio stations playing my songs or taking them off their playlists. I was leaning in to him in a fresh way, one that wasn't contingent on performance or reputation.

Time had for many years been the thing I was always fighting and chasing, trying to cram more things into the day—more recording, more tour dates, more modeling and advertising gigs, more, more, more. Time flew and whirled under the wheels of the tour bus and through the engines of the airplanes I seemed to be on constantly. Hurried and harried, I'd been wrestling the arms of the clock.

Now, time slowed and ambled. I was still doing one-offs: trips to Singapore or Argentina to perform. But I wasn't on the road continually. There was time to read. Time to walk. Time to wander. Time to wonder. Time to stroll through museums. Time to sit and watch the Thames slip along its ancient banks; time to watch the English oaks begin to change color slowly in September and slide into what the Brits call "full tinting," that blaze of reds and golds, in October.

God was repurposing time for me, showing me shades of sabbath by slowing my seasons.

So I learned Spanish in London. And I learned to cook. And I learned how to be a daughter again, both a daughter to my mom and a daughter of the King.

London is six hours ahead of Nashville. And in this new season of alone for me, I needed to learn how to take care of myself. So, a little before dinnertime in London, I would Skype my mom, which was just a little before lunchtime in Nashville. Over that scratchy audio and video signal, my mom would guide me and show me how to prepare various recipes.

God was repurposing time for my mom and me, letting us have time as a mother and daughter, a mom showing her girl how to cook, how to navigate the kitchen. It was time we hadn't had when I was growing up because we were zipping from town to town and eating the well-meaning and endless casseroles brought by the ladies of whichever church we were singing at. Then, as the recording contracts came in and my schedule and career became the focus of family life, there had been no time to function as mother and daughter; we were then manager and talent. There hadn't been time to learn and receive from my mom the skills and heirloom kind of wisdom of making a home.

Then my parents divorced. In the months leading up to their divorce and in the aftermath of what that meant in our family life, I'd had to grow up fast. I became the family peacemaker in addition to being the breadwinner. That season had displaced what for most people is a time when they gently launch out from their parents' homes into the first stages of their adult lives. My parents' divorce catapulted my relationships with them into unfamiliar territory, as they were both processing and trying to heal.

But now, across an ocean and with six hours of daylight between us, God was repurposing time and resetting the clock.

God was giving my mom and me that time back, time to connect, time to hand down recipes. Time to talk about something completely other than my music and choices and career. He was showing me how he can reset time in a literal way as the time difference between London and Nashville was creating powerful moments for the relationship between my mom and me. This time when we were separated by an ocean was bringing us together in relationship. This time difference between the two continents was something God was using to allow us a fresh season.

We'd connect each day online. She'd give me some ideas for upcoming meals. She'd give me some items to put on my shopping list. She'd walk me through recipes, show me the techniques she used for chopping and sautéing and seasoning and baking. She'd tell me the stories behind some of the recipes, the ones that had been handed down to her by her mom or her grandma. She'd explain how to find the best ingredients, what to watch out for to avoid overcooking a dish. Even though I'd been living with my mom through the years, I was now being given the time to get to know her more, on a deeper level, through our computers and those pixelated videos.

There is a passage of Scripture that gets quoted a whole bunch, but I think it's because it resonates so deeply with us, with this glimpse we have of God who owns time and uses it for our good. King Solomon, as he was looking back on the pages of his life, reflected on the purpose of time and seasons in our lives. He wrote,

> There is a time for everything, and a season for every activity under the heavens: a time to be born and a time to die, a time to plant and a time to uproot, a time to kill and a time to heal, a time to tear down and a time to build, a time to weep and a time to laugh, a time to mourn and a time to dance, a time to scatter stones and a time to gather them, a time to embrace and a time to refrain from embracing, a time to search and a time to give up, a time to keep and a time to throw away, a time to tear and a time to mend, a time to be silent and a time to speak, a time to love and a time to hate, a time for war and a time for peace. (Ecc. 3:1–8)

And a time to Skype and a time to cook.
Praise be to the God who resets time.

• • •

The year I spent in London was drawing to a close. There was something on the horizon that I needed to take care of. Back when my first marriage was heading off the embankment, back when tour dates were getting thin after the release of *Papi*, doctors had discovered I had polyps on my vocal cords. They can be pretty common among singers, and they show up when you've overused your voice or you've been singing in a way that stresses the vocal cords too much. It's like when you rub a callus on your foot from those heels you love to wear over and over but they don't love you back. On your vocal cords, those calluses can lead to your voice sounding hoarser, and they can begin to limit your singing range or cause your voice to break at the most inopportune times during a song. My doctor had recommended that I have surgery to remove the polyps before I even left for London, but I'd put it off, feeling like too many other things were urgent and in crisis mode.

But now it was time to come home. Time to face what I'd run away from. Time to determine next steps and who I wanted to be.

I came back to the States in the late fall and made the appointment for the surgery. It seemed like everything around my singing was in jeopardy. From my messed-up reputation to the actual health of my throat, it was all on the bubble. I knew there were risks to having the surgery, not the least of which was that I could end up with permanent damage to my vocal cords and never sound or sing the same way again. But the risk of not having the surgery was more significant, and so I got ready to undergo the procedure.

Those months in London, hanging out online with Mom, came back into play when I had the surgery. I wanted to be with my mom. I wanted her to take care of me. I wanted to be at her house, let her bring me smoothies and soft foods, and simply be her little girl. And she gave that to me. Following the surgery, I got myself tucked in at my mom's house and hunkered down for eight weeks of a compulsory vow of silence.

I'd love to tell you that I used that time in a super spiritual way, that I found something mystic and deep in being quiet for the first time in my life, that I walked away with some huge revelation about being speechless. That I learned a fresh way to listen. But that would be a lie. Instead I watched movies—I know you're shocked. What, Jaci? You? You watched tons of movies?

Look, I'm nothing if not on-brand.

But it was another way God reset time. From the time I was little, so much of my worth had been wrapped up in the sound I could make. I had associated my value with the vocal communication gift that God had given me. But now, I wasn't able to make a sound. Not a peep. And I wasn't even doing something amazing with that time, just watching movies like *Gone with the Wind* over and over.

And guess what?

God still loved me. Still provided for me. I had nothing to prove to him. And he was gracious enough to simply let me heal in silence. I got to go back to that place of being a baby girl in his presence, nothing to offer, simply eating and napping and receiving the care of my mom. I had no witty zingers to give, no song to sing. I just ate ice cream, watched movies, and let the clock tick. I learned to simply let the moments flow. Getting antsy about wanting those recovery weeks to go fast wouldn't make them go any faster. There was a beauty in just letting time *be*. No need to chase it, no need to manage it, no need to fight it. Just let it ticktock. And heal.

. . .

God does reset time from time to time. See what I did there? But he does. For his purpose.

Joshua was a warrior of a guy. He and Caleb were the two

spies who peeked over in the promised land and figured with a macho faith they could take the giants in the land. The other ten guys with them weren't so confident. As in, they said it couldn't be done. But Joshua and Caleb finally had their shot after years of wandering in the wilderness, and Joshua wasn't about to back down. Joshua had been kicking tail and taking names when he got into the promised land of Canaan, and he'd made lots of kings in the area nervous. When a particular group of kings heard that he might be heading their way, they decided to make an alliance and create a super army to try to man up against Joshua. It all reached a full boil when the armies began to battle. They fought all day, and then something amazing happened.

Joshua said to the LORD in the presence of Israel:

> "Sun, stand still over Gibeon,
>   and you, moon, over the Valley of Aijalon."
> So the sun stood still,
>   and the moon stopped,
>   till the nation avenged itself on its enemies. . . .

The sun stopped in the middle of the sky and delayed going down about a full day. There has never been a day like it before or since, a day when the LORD listened to a human being. Surely the LORD was fighting for Israel! (Josh. 10:12–14)

Some people say it was an eclipse; others have different explanations. Here's what I know: God repurposed time so Joshua could fight his enemies.

And I think he can do that for us when we are battling, when we are fighting to live out our purpose, when we are challenged.

It probably won't be whatever cool cosmic galaxy thing he did for Joshua, but he can mold it and meld it in ways that we can't understand.

Psalm 90:4 gives us some hints about God and time. It says, "A thousand years in your sight are like a day that has just gone by, or like a watch in the night." I can find all through the Bible places where people thought God was taking far too long. And I can find places where he shows up suddenly. And it doesn't always gel with my idea of how long things should take or how quickly I want answers.

But at the end of the day, he rules the clock. And he has perfect timing.

• • •

What is an issue for you? Do you feel like God is late in answering your prayers? Do you feel like he's taking his time, and it's making you doubt if he'll ever show up? Or are you trying to speed through a trying season, trying to get it over with and out of the way? I get it. I really do. But there's this really beautiful thing that can happen if we'll just lean in to whatever pace God is setting: it puts the clock back in its rightful place, not as our master. And catch this: it's not our job to master the clock. God is *over* time. He is the master of how it all ticks. And when we can get to that place, where we're not chasing the clock and it's not chasing us, we can embrace and enjoy where God has us, what he's teaching us in this moment, on this day.

Sometimes, just like Joshua, the daylight will be extended on a battle. I've asked the question, and you probably have, too, *God, can't we just wrap this up? I mean, this super daylight saving time thing is cool and all, but seriously. Can't we just be*

Catch this: it's not our job to *master the clock*. God is over time. He is the master of how it all ticks.

• • •

learned in that longer day. I'm encouraged that he stayed in the battle for however long it took, and God provided the light to do that. Joshua asked the master of the clock to make time bend to a greater purpose. And God did it.

done already? But then, I look at how much more endurance Joshua built during that reset of time. I look at how much he

I went to London to learn Spanish. I came home to learn to be silent. And in all of it, I learned this:

My times are in your hands.

PSALM 31:15

And you, my friend, you can learn this too. Stop watching your watch. And watch what God will do.

Flip the Script

- Do you feel like you're always fighting the clock? What's behind that? What are you afraid of? We live in a culture that makes us think that we have to accomplish certain things by certain times or we will have missed our shot. But is that true?

- What treasures have you gained in a time of waiting? What were your emotions during that time? I used to hate, hate, hate having to wait in a dentist's office or airport. But I'm trying to lean in now. I'm trying to see it as "found" time, the opportunity to pick up that book I haven't had time to get to and read, a chance to simply sit and be in the moment. How could you change the way you look at a waiting time?

- What are some times in your life you can look back on now and see that God was up to something completely different from what you thought was going on? How did God repurpose that time for you?

Seven

Never Too Late

In the Nic of Time

I was sitting on the potty.

That's how all great romance stories should begin. Don't you think?

But I was. Really. And my cell phone began to ring. It was a 512 area code and it didn't show as any of my contacts. I almost didn't pick up. But I did. There was just one person I used to know with a 512 area code. And he was long past speaking to me. But just in case, I answered.

And this is what I heard: "When are you going to leave all those bad boys and come back to me?" And then a familiar laugh. It was Nic Gonzales, the guy whose heart I had broken after making *Chasing Papi*.

I was in Florida, about to hit the stage to sing at a festival. I'd come through my vocal cord surgery and had healed well, with virtually no change to my voice tone or quality. While I didn't know yet if or when I'd be recording next, I was still receiving the opportunity to play at various events and festivals, hence this particular trip to Florida. Nic had been playing at the same festival, but a couple of days earlier. He'd seen my name on the posters and decided to give me a call. He was already back home in Austin but knew I'd be in Florida for the show. We were two ships in the night for that Florida date, which was how it had been for us for a number of years. Two people who just kept seeming to miss each other.

I thought it was a little odd for him to call. Nice and all, but weird. After all, it hadn't ended well between us. And it wasn't just the breakup. The last time I'd been around him, after the breakup, after I'd gotten married, we'd had a truly cringeworthy encounter.

I had been trying to salvage my contemporary Christian music career after all the criticism from the movie, still thinking that perhaps my wedding would do the trick. A tour was put together for me, a three-month, multistate tour. The organizers had set up a couple of bands as the openers for each date, and one of those bands was—wait for it—Salvador.

Yeah. Nic's band. The band he was the lead singer for. *That* band. The band of my ex-boyfriend. That band.

I know. Let's all get it out of our systems with a collective groan.

I knew it would be a little awkward, but in many ways, I also didn't think it would be a big deal. I'd had lots of boyfriends. I was sure to encounter them from time to time. And now I was a married woman, so surely everyone had moved on. Like, whatever, right?

So here we were on tour together, a few years and my new marriage between us. It really didn't bother me to be around Nic. It felt . . . neutral. But as the tour kicked off, I couldn't figure something out.

He was rude to me. I mean, legit rude.

At the conclusion of each concert, all the band members from each group were supposed to come and sing my final song with me. Nic always found a reason to not come out. We'd be standing in a catering room, and he'd act like he didn't see me. I'd speak to him, and he would literally stare past me and not respond, seemingly not hearing or seeing me. He ignored, avoided, and generally glared at me with this empty yet ambivalent look. It was bizarre. And rude. After all, this was *my* tour! I was the headliner! Hello!

Well, fine. I figured I would just keep being me and he could just deal. It was only three months, after all. (I would later learn that what I was interpreting as "rude" was actually an extremely noble respect. But it would be a good long time before I figured that out.)

But then it wasn't three months. The tour was faltering. Organizers were backing out in city after city, the fallout of my movie role and my controversial marriage slopping doubt onto the best-laid plans. The crowds at the dates we were playing weren't what we'd hoped for. The tour just wasn't working, and the reaction to my movie role and quickie marriage was much worse than my managers or I had ever expected. We staggered through a month or so, but then all the dates dried up. We had to shutter the tour early, so Nic and I parted ways again, the sour sting of a failed tour to add to all the awkward.

It had been more than three years since I'd last seen him, almost five years since I'd broken up with him. Why in the world was he calling me now?

"Can I take you to dinner?" he asked.

Um, okay.

"Well, I'm obviously not in Nashville right now," I said. "And you're in Austin. I'll be back in Nashville tomorrow. So . . . tomorrow night?"

I could hear Nic's smile through the cell signal. "Can't be there tomorrow, but I can be there Tuesday. Does that work?"

I agreed, chatted with him for a couple more minutes, then hung up. Well, *that was interesting.*

He showed up in Nashville the next Tuesday, took me to dinner, made me laugh, caught me up on his life. It was fine.

Fine. But not sparks. Just good old Nic. Nic and Jaci, out for a friendly dinner, two old acquaintances catching up. He flew home to Austin. That was that.

And then he called again. And showed up again. And took me to dinner again.

Okay. Fine. Whatever.

And then again.

But I was holding him at arm's length. Even with my time in London, even with some perspective and some humility on me, I wasn't thinking falling in love was on the menu for me for a while. I was still trying to figure out what to do with my rocky career path. I was just getting over a major throat surgery. And, at the end of the day, I just didn't feel for Nic what he seemed to feel for me.

Until.

Nic showed up yet again in Nashville one weekend. I figured it would be a visit like the previous ones, a nice dinner, some chitchat, and then he'd head back to Texas. We were sitting at an awesome restaurant here in Nashville called Tayst. It's since closed, but it was one of my favorite spots, a small place with a swooping chocolate-and-tan-striped awning on the front of the building, close to downtown. It held just a few tables and boasted an exquisite menu, lots of little courses with food creations that looked like plate-size pieces of art. We'd been seeing each other quite a bit, Nic flying in from Austin to take me to dinner and to see me. I'd enjoyed the time together, but I still didn't think this was going to turn into anything on my part. I had a whole bunch of reasons why I didn't think the friendship between Nic and me was going to go any further.

And then God hijacked my heart.

Well, God and Nic's ridiculous eyelashes. Nic has the kind of eyelashes women go get expensive extensions to have. The kind that cost you serious money. Nic just grows them. Out of his eyelids. For *free*! *Grrrrr* . . . And he knows how to use them on me.

So there we were, having this friendly dinner at Tayst. And we're chatting and I'm telling stories, and Nic's laughing and he's adding in some stories of his own, and the whole time he's batting those eyelashes at me. In a manly way. But still.

And all of a sudden, there it was. The zing. The connection. The moment. It just all connected, in a way it hadn't before for me. It all just became . . . clear. I could see it. I could see what God had intended all along.

I was meant to be with this man, this man who had loved me and prayed for me and let me go and then was willing to put his heart out there again.

Who does that?

Nic loved me with the kind of love that doesn't give up. Loved me enough to call me on my stuff. Loved me enough to let me break up with him over it. Loved me enough to love me fully when I was only willing to risk a little crush on him. Loved me enough to be cold to me when I was off-limits during my first marriage.

Loved me enough to swallow his pride and call me out of the blue when I was damaged goods in the eyes of the world, when I had nothing to offer.

We sat in that restaurant, at one of those small tables down that single aisle of the dining room, chocolate-brown napkins draped across our laps, small plates of pretty bites being brought out in a well-timed choreography, and I fell. Hard. Just like that. No one was more surprised than me.

I was meant to be *with this man*, this man who had loved me and prayed for me and let me go and then was willing to put his heart out there again.

Now I can look back and see it. Nic had always represented a scary place for me. Not Nic himself. He's always been a rock, been a place of safety and rest. But he's also bold and he loved me beyond the accolades and recording contracts. He was self-assured and had his own music career. He had been willing to tell me what I didn't want to hear. He was the person so many people in my world had thought I should be with. But that would mean I wasn't in control, and control was what I craved.

Sometimes the greatest act of courage is to surrender.

To love Nic, I had to let go of that desire to control, that greed to be the one leading the orchestra of the various players in my life. To love Nic, I had to let go of trying to form him, conform him to me. I think I knew somewhere deep down he wouldn't let that happen anyway, but it was important for it to be a conscious decision on my part, to embrace Nic for who he was and not to always be trying to adjust it. I had to learn the beauty of leaning in to the whole of who someone was, not what he could do for me, not how he could play a role in my life, but to build a life with him, the totalities of each of us brought to the table.

When we've been hurt, when we've been sideswiped by life, we make ourselves all kinds of promises, don't we?

"I'll never let anyone hurt me like that again."
"I'll never trust anyone again."
"I'll never put myself out there like that again."

We scramble for what we see as control because we think it's the loss of control that wounded us. Control isn't really about control; it's about fear. That's what I've been learning in my morning Bible study recently with some girls in my neighborhood. At the very center of all that control I was desperately using, from trying to pull control from those around me to making controversial career decisions, to trying to fix messes I'd made, to deciding to avoid other messes by exerting even more control in new relationships and career choices, right down at the bottom of all that was fear.

I still wrestle with those tendencies today. But God is repurposing that feeling for me. When I feel that rising sense of panic, that place where I want to grab the wheel of life and start telling people off and start shutting down, he's reminding me to lean in. He's teaching me that feelings can be a signal that, really, I'm feeling vulnerable, not powerful. And he whispers to me anew that, in him, there's no "too late." After all, he came up with this whole concept of time. And he's the only one who gets to decide when time is done. It's only when he says "It is finished" that counts. As long as he has you here, as long as he has me here, there is still time.

Once it clicked for me with Nic, time sped up. Really sped up. Within a few short months, things were serious. Real serious. Out of honor, Nic approached my dad and asked permission to marry me. And right after my dad gave his blessing, Nic took a knee on the light carpet in front of my white suede couch in my cool downtown condo and asked me to be his wife. Three weeks later, I flew into Austin, went to the venue we'd picked out, and married Nic. Simple, sweet, quiet, with people we loved in attendance, a little cake and punch reception. Profound.

Understandably, Nic had people in his world who were concerned. Actually, they were super concerned. Let's face it, I was now a woman with a not-all-that-distant past. I had a divorce under my belt. I was a child of divorce, with parents who had each had several failed marriages between them, including their own. But Nic was firm with those who had their concerns. He said in an interview with *Crosswalk*:

> I've lived my life with a lot of amazing grace that's been given to me. People have given me the benefit of the doubt my whole life. And I realized that in my lifetime, if I can't extend that same grace to someone—to people around me, my peers, and now my wife—then I would consider that to be hypocrisy at its best. I realized that I didn't love Jaci for her career, or for her past. And I also didn't want to be the person to sit around and go, "Oh, that person is not qualified for me." Who am I to say? I'm not sinless. I've made mistakes. All I knew was I really liked being around Jaci. I was in love with her and she's become my best friend. Regardless of what happened, that was yesterday; that's not important to me. I believe that I'm strong enough in my own faith and strong enough as a husband to say that it's all okay. And if other people are unforgiving, that's not a problem. Because of the grace that I'm extended, I know that we're both going to be okay.[5]

I asked him one day after we were married why he'd been so cold to me during that failed tour years ago, that attitude I'd interpreted as rude, in that awkward time when I was in a doomed, reactive marriage and he was my old boyfriend who'd gotten dumped. He looked at me incredulously. "Well, Jaci," he said, "I couldn't be in love with you. You were married to someone else." And he couldn't be apathetic. So *aloof* was all that was left. Like they say, there's a thin line between love and hate. Nic was exhibiting the highest form of respect in staying clear of me.

Even through failure, even through bad decisions, even through missed opportunities, God can make "wrong" and "too late" into "right" and "right now." God showed up in the Nic of time.

• • •

Do you have a season in your life that feels like it was just wasted years? Are you in one right now? Time that could have been so much more fruitful, so much better, if you just hadn't blown it on running, hiding, whatever your particular issue? Or maybe it's nothing that you did, it's just the way life worked out, the person you loved walked out, the dream job went south. It's so easy to focus on regret when you've got that kind of season in your history or in your today. And when we focus on regret, it can paralyze us from moving forward.

Do you feel like it's too late? That opportunity, that relationship, that moment, that you'll never get that chance again?

Listen. God can repurpose your remorse. I can't promise that the romance with the one who got away will circle back. I can't promise that the job opportunity you walked away from will open back up. I can't promise that you'll be able to fix the relationship with that friend that ended in a blaze of thunderbolts of misunderstanding and anger.

But what I do know is that when we take the walk of repentance, God can rescript our "too late" into "never too late." His ability to renew and recover isn't dependent on our human timetable.

Now hear me good, girl. When I say the walk of repentance, I'm not talking about that walk of shame. I'm not talking about a walk down to the front of the church at the end of a church service. I'm talking about a walk of repentance in which we own our part of the mess of what seems like wasted years, even if it's simply that we didn't take the chance or we chose the wrong person to be in relationship with. I'm talking about cultivating the lessons from that time. There can be fruit even in a season of drought. That can sound counterintuitive, but there really can be fruit there. Okay, maybe more like root vegetables. Things that are good for you but maybe don't taste as good and sweet as fruit. Like beets. Good for you. Nutritional. But you may have to dig for them. You will probably get dirty. You'll get grime under your nails, and you'll wonder if the nutrition of that spiritual veggie is worth the feel on your teeth.

And it is. It is.

It's not about beating yourself up. Beating yourself up isn't progress. It's about stopping the whole looking-over-your-shoulder thing and seeing what God has next. Being open to it. Vulnerably taking up a scared courage and turning the calendar to a fresh page.

Those spiritual veggies? They may not be as sweet as strawberries. But they don't have to be bitter.

Bitterness is another place we can get stuck in the gorge of regret. And here's the deal with bitterness. It sometimes sounds and feels like wisdom. Believe me, while I was heartbroken over my failed marriage, it seemed only wise to swear off men, to shut down coffee dates with a quick stir of disinterest. I had no business dating since my track record was now a solid fail. Men couldn't be trusted. Men could hurt you beyond comprehension. Men could make all kinds of promises and walk away. So stay away from men. Smart, right?

It was bitterness holding me back. Not wisdom.

It makes me think about Naomi. We read about her in the book of Ruth. She had married a local Bethlehem boy and had a couple of kids. Then famine hit, and she and her husband packed the kids into whatever would have been a Hebrew U-Haul and headed for Moab, hoping that groceries and work would be more plentiful there. They stayed there for several years, her boys growing into men and marrying girls from Moab.

And then the unexpected happened. The script she'd been living, the one featuring the comfortable life in Moab, was erased. Her husband and her sons all died. She was left in a strange land with nothing familiar except for the foreign brides her sons left behind. Lonely. Hurt. Confused. Sad.

She decided to head back to her homeland, and her daughters-in-law signed up to go with her. Ultimately, only one daughter-in-law remained with her on the long trek home: Ruth. When they arrived back in the Bethlehem region, Naomi's family went out to greet her, to welcome her home, calling her name.

She was not having it. Check out this socially awkward moment, recorded in the first chapter of the book of Ruth:

> So the two women went on until they came to Bethlehem. When they arrived in Bethlehem, the whole town was stirred because of them, and the women exclaimed, "Can this be Naomi?"

"Don't call me Naomi," she told them. "Call me Mara, because the Almighty has made my life very bitter. I went away full, but the LORD has brought me back empty. Why call me Naomi? The LORD has afflicted me; the Almighty has brought misfortune upon me." (vv. 19–21)

Um, yeah. That's sounds like a great way to renew friendships when you arrive back in your hometown after years away. She wanted them to call her *Mara*, which means, you guessed it, "bitter."

Naomi means "pleasantness," but life had dog-piled on her and left its stamp on her heart. She was blaming God, she was building up armor, she was skidding into town with a vapor trail of hurt in her wake. You know, I understand. I really do. She didn't want to get hurt again. And sometimes, when we don't want to get hurt again, we trade in hope for bitterness.

But here's what's interesting. Apparently, the townspeople never did take to calling her by this new name. For the rest of the book, whenever she's referred to, it's always as Naomi, "pleasant," instead of Mara, "bitter." I wonder if she was bitter about *that* (see what I did there?).

Don't miss this: There's the rest of the book. She came back into town assuming her story had been fully written. But there were more pages to follow. Ruth proved herself a devoted and loving daughter-in-law, certainly not a replacement for the sons Naomi had lost, but still a person willing to love and serve Naomi with the devotion and honor of a child to a mother. Naomi didn't find a new husband, but she did find a new husband for Ruth in Boaz, a man who welcomed Naomi into his family as a mother-in-law, giving her a place of covering and provision. He didn't simply marry Ruth and write off Naomi, trafficking in the technicality that Ruth and Naomi weren't blood related. He took them as a package deal, embracing Naomi as grandmother to the child he and Ruth bore, to the point that the women of the town reminded her, "Praise be to the LORD, who this day has not left you without a guardian-redeemer. May he become famous throughout Israel! He will renew your life and sustain you in your old age. For your daughter-in-law, who loves you and who is better to you than seven sons, has given him birth" (4:14–15).

With God, it's never too late. He can't be late: he invented this whole idea of time, which gives him lots of wiggle room to use time any way he wants. And that includes that he gets to decide what is right on time. Let me tell you what that season of lost years can become in the hands of God. Check out these promises:

> "I will restore to you the years that the swarming locust has eaten." (Joel 2:25 NKJV)
>
> "Then you shall know that I am in the midst of Israel: I am the LORD your God." (Joel 2:27 NKJV)
>
> "GOD, your God, will restore everything you lost; he'll have compassion on you; he'll come back and pick up the pieces from all the places where you were scattered. No matter how far away you end up, GOD, your God, will get you out of there and bring you back to the land your ancestors once possessed. It will be yours again. He will give you a good life and make you more numerous than your ancestors. GOD, your God, will cut away the thick calluses on your heart and your children's hearts, freeing you to love GOD, your God, with your whole heart and soul and live, really live. GOD, your God, will put all these curses on your enemies who hated you and were out to get you. And you will make a new start, listening

obediently to GOD, keeping all his commandments that I'm commanding you today. GOD, your God, will outdo himself in making things go well for you." (Deut. 30:5–8 THE MESSAGE)

Here's another way we can cooperate with God in redeeming lost time for us: retrospection. Retrospection is the ability to look back on what has happened and glean the wisdom from it. Retrospection is not regret. It's not a call back to longing for something that's gone or obsessing over what went wrong. It's simply noting the good and the bad of that season, how it's shaped you, and what you could have done better, without becoming bitter.

• • •

In the Nic of time, I've learned that it's never too late. You know, in all the history Nic and I had before getting married, Nic could have been bitter. He chose better. Nic could have beaten himself up. Instead, he chose to build, building up reserves of patience and understanding and grace. Nic could have blocked me from his contact list, from his professional life, from his heart. Instead, he took the risk to unlock me, to lovingly accept all my mess and not allow the ravages of the clock and my choices to cancel out our future.

Today, all these years later, plenty of history and mistakes and joys and laughter and tears in our wake, he hands me the razor he uses for his face for me to shave my legs. True love. And that's what it's really about, isn't it? When we use a razor to scrape the scruff from our hearts, we don't wield it as a weapon toward those we love, but rather extend it, handle first, to the people who are most important to us. We show them we are willing to go first, to take the risk to be naked and vulnerable, bare from a beard of bitter, and to try again. And God will meet us there, making what we thought was too late arrive just on time.

Flip the Script

- What is something in your life that feels like it's "too late"? It's a particularly hard thing when we know that this side of eternity there isn't a chance at reconciliation or forgiveness. But without oversimplifying things, what is something you could do to release that person or situation that hurt you, or whom you hurt, and now can't mend it? How can you release yourself from all that and be ready and wiser when God brings new opportunity or relationship to your life?

- Do you sometimes cling to a "too late" attitude out of stubbornness? I know I did. Do you know the why behind that stubbornness? Does it make you feel more powerful, make you feel like you've inoculated yourself against a further hurt? I get it. I really do. But have you considered what that stubbornness just might cost you? Is that a price you're willing to pay? Think about the message of Psalm 81:

> So I gave them over to their stubborn hearts
>   to follow their own devices.
> "If my people would only listen to me,
>   if Israel would only follow my ways,
> how quickly I would subdue their enemies
>   and turn my hand against their foes!

Those who hate the LORD would cringe before him,
    and their punishment would last forever.
But you would be fed with the finest of wheat;
    with honey from the rock I would satisfy you."

(VV. 12–16)

- Girlfriend, I want you to have everything God has for you, the "finest of wheat" and the "honey from the rock." What steps can you take to trust him with your next steps, your next days? People will disappoint, circumstances will change, but God can be there with you and for you, if you'll let him.

- Think about this quote: "It's never too late to become who you might have been." Do you agree or disagree? Do you think God can make you into all he intended, even if you think the season has passed?

Eight

It's Personal

Genevieve. JoJo. Sarah. Lauren. They're my girls. We do a lot of life together. We're together all the time. I've known them since they were cute toddlers and awkward teenagers, and now, as grown-up girls, I've seen a couple of them through some difficult deliveries. I depend on them and they depend on me.

Hank. Darth. Chubby. Chunky. Day Day. Pierre. LK Junior.

They're also my girls. Yep. Even Pierre. All of them, the whole lot, the ones with girl names and the ones whose names are more, um, descriptive, they're all mine.

Chickens.

Hens, to be precise.

If you had told me back in my downtown loft-living days that there would come a time when I would turn into a crazy chicken lady, I would have never, ever believed you. I thought I was City Mouse all the way.

Turns out, I'm Country Mouse too. Loft to the coop, it's been a ride.

If you were over for coffee, we'd sit at my long white dining table positioned near the long white sectional and you would think you were back at my downtown loft. City Mouse. And then we'd walk outside.

And you'd see the most intense country chicken habitat ever for my girls.

I'm chicken obsessed. Country Mouse all the way. Silver Laced Wyandotte. Ameraucana. Barred Rock. Amber Link. Black Australorp. Golden Comet. These are important names to me: the breeds of my girls and all the unique attributes they carry.

It all started innocently enough. When we moved to our fixer-upper of a home, nestled on three acres outside of Nashville, tucked back under towering green trees and surrounded by a sagging old fence, it seemed like there should be some kind of pet to go along with the new house. But the dog thing and the cat thing didn't really appeal to me. I didn't really want animals in my house given that I was already living with three human males—that seemed animal enough to me. And I for sure didn't want some kind of rodent or reptile in a plastic crate living in the basement, nocturnal and creepy, running on a wheel or slithering under a heat lamp. Blergh. Shiver. Ugh.

But I digress.

This house was an ultimate DIY kind of purchase. From the front door to the back and all points in between, we've sanded, painted, torn out, built back, and more. We've learned more about foundations and Sheetrock and caulking and plumbing than could be covered in an evening of HGTV. It's been an ongoing labor of love (and sometimes hate).

I'd make a run to the hardware store for yet more supplies for our seemingly endless renovation projects. The perfume of ply-wood and paint always gets my possibilities juices flowing, and I wandered the aisles, making sure I'd gotten what was on my list and taking in the latest upgrade options for bathroom sinks and what the new sexy is in sump pumps. And I don't mean pumps as in shoes. I mean pumps as in making sure your basement doesn't flood kind of pumps. Sump pumps . . . 'cuz country living.

And then I saw it.

On sale.

A chicken tractor.

I know. You've been tempted before, too, right? Or maybe it's just me?

"What's a chicken tractor?" you may ask. Well, it's kind of like a poultry RV. It's a small enclosure made of—wait for it—chicken wire. You can easily move it around your yard on its wheels, relocating your chickens if they get tired of the view. It's sort of a low-commitment chicken trial kit. Kind of. You're not doing anything permanent. It's a chicken test drive, for pity's sake. It wouldn't make me a long-term kind of hen lady.

It's for the kids.

It will be good for them.

It will teach them responsibility.

These are all the things I told myself as I went completely rogue on my simple hardware shopping list and brought home an on-sale chicken tractor.

I can already hear your next question.

I understand. I really do. I was right where you may be now just a few short years ago. The chicken uninitiated.

Where do you get chickens for the chicken tractor? Valid question.

The mail. Kid you not.

You order them online. This is really a thing. You hop on the chicken website of your choice, put in your order for day-old chicks, and they arrive priority mail.

Seriously. I like to think that I've spiced up my mailman's life just a little bit.

I started off small. Just the chicken tractor and three or four day-old baby chicks by mail. We kept them fed. Kept them in the chicken tractor, cute little bits of yellow fluff running around in the tractor confines.

And they grew. And then my boys Zealand and Søren started showing great responsibility in feeding and watering them. And the chicks grew some more. And I started doing more research on chickens. And I developed a wish list for my next round of chicken collecting.

"Ooohhhh. A Blue Copper Maran. I *need* one of those! Ha! And a Mille Fleur d'Uccle. Why, those were the hens of queens! I've got to find one of those."

(For real. According to chicken legend, there was a queen who liked to hold one of these little hens because the hen's feathers made it look like the queen was holding "one thousand flowers," which is what *mille fleur* means. Chicken trivia rocks.)

Over time, my chicken collection became larger. By a lot. And I then learned this truth: when you develop a chicken habit, your chicken habitat also needs to grow. So after about nine months of chicken tractor life, it was time to make the big leap.

Yep. All the way to coop. And not just any coop. Not for my girls. I wanted them to have plenty of play area. I wanted it to be secure. I wanted it to have different options, with a nice bank of private chicken condos at one end and plenty of public gathering space for hen parties. I wanted it to have soaring ceilings, yes, made of chicken wire, but still. And I wanted it to have plenty of room to house a whole bunch of hens because I was capon shopping.

And so the Hen Hacienda was born. Some people say they're house poor. I say I'm coop rich.

It really is a thing of beauty, our coop, with plenty of hen amenities. And once we got it built, I began building my chicken family to include all kinds of exotic breeds, like the Golden Comet and the Ancona. And of course I needed a White Crested Black Polish—they've got this over-the-top messy bun that looks like blonde Texas big hair with dark roots. It's an homage to my birthplace. Google 'em: White Crested Black Polish. It's worth your time, I promise.

The girls now give us twelve to sixteen eggs a day, in a variety of shapes and colors, everything from a deep chocolate brown to a sky blue. Zealand and Søren dutifully feed them morning and night, refilling their water, talking to them, chasing them, adoring them. I'll sit at that long, white, modern dining table, drinking black coffee out of a white porcelain mug, staring out the window at my boys taking care of our messy, hilarious, colorful chickens, and I'll laugh to myself. Because I now know these chickens like I know my boys. I know which ones are shier and which ones are bolder. I know the ones who like me best, or who follow after Zealand, or who have made Søren their person. I know which of the hens are just fine if they seem a little quiet, and I know which ones I should be worried about if they don't come out to meet me when I amble out to the coop. They each have their own little personalities.

Chickens. Who would have thought? Some of them look a lot alike, but I can tell them apart because of their temperaments. I'm reminded afresh that God makes all of his creatures so unique, so fascinating. That's why my relationship with each of my hens is personal. In a chicken kind of way. I really do enjoy getting to know each of those little chicks that arrive in the mail and seeing who they turn into, how they get along with the others, how their little quirks and idiosyncrasies add to the whole flavor of the coop.

But then I have to sit back and wonder. I'm so accepting of these chickens. I really delight in getting to know them, in learning their little individualities. I don't feel some need to "fix" any of the chickens; I just like getting to know them for who they are. Chickens, for heaven's sake. So why, truly for heaven's sake, have I had such a hard time accepting my own personality, quirks, and temperament? Why did I for so long try to be what everyone else thought I should be?

God sure does have a funny way with personalities. And he's teaching me some things about being intentional with how he created me, for his sake, instead of just letting life happen to me and accepting narrow definitions.

• • •

As a girl who really loves black and white, I get it—I really do. It's not just decor that looks great in a black-and-white palette. Life can seem a lot cleaner when we quickly decide to categorize people and places and events and politics and hard topics. It keeps the dust and fuss down to a minimum. It makes us feel better when we don't have to deal with things that feel uncertain or unknown. We get a few details, assign them a place in our hearts and heads, and move on.

We decide that someone who is funny at all the parties must be hilarious and never have a down day. We decide that someone who seems hesitant doesn't have courage. We categorize a woman dressed to the nines as someone who has it all together. We decide that our neighbor we never see out of sweats and an old resort T-shirt isn't all that driven.

But guess what? That funny person at the party may deal with periods of depression. That hesitant person could be the bravest one in the room because they evaluate and consider their decisions and then take decisive action. That woman dressed to the nines may have an inner life racked with self-doubt. That sweats-clad neighbor just might be the gazillionaire owner of a tech firm.

We limit our understanding of who people are, who they truly are and how they fit in our paradigms, based on a few pieces of information. And that limiting can rob us of friendships that could have been fascinating and powerful if we'd just dropped our assumptions.

The relationship where we tend to do it the most? For many of us, it's the relationship with ourselves. We cling to what others have told us about ourselves. We reach for the expectations others have. We press ourselves into tight sleeves of stereotypes, longing for a sense of belonging and place.

And then we resent it, that we don't feel truly seen. Seen for who we really are and how we really tick.

But if we want to be seen and known, we have to first take a real look at ourselves.

. . .

Because I came into all the entertainer and performer hype so early in my life, the search for my truest personality and self was a meandering one. And when I talk with my girlfriends today, even those who had what we might call far more normal child-hoods than mine, I discover that many of them also had people and situations playing into how they saw themselves. They also struggled to find their "place."

It's that irony I've found over and over in my life and with my friends. We all want to be unique. And we don't want to be left out.

When Nic and I moved to the country, it didn't seem to fit with what my family and friends thought they knew about me. They know that I really do love urban settings, big cities, hustle and bustle, modern settings, and monochromatic cool clothes, which is why so many of them found it absolutely hilarious when Nic and I started looking for a house with a yard and a fence and big trees. Heck, it didn't seem to fit with what *I* thought I knew about myself. And as sure as I was about wanting to raise my kids with room to run, I wasn't sure I wanted to give up that modern career-girl persona, to the point that we kept the downtown townhouse as a rental property, just in case. Never mind that it was all glass and chrome and stairs and one bedroom and hardly the kind of place to house toddlers safely.

It felt like I was having to choose between two versions of myself, that I needed to commit to one or the other. City Mouse? Or Country Mouse? Because somewhere, I thought it wasn't valid to be both. I thought I had to choose one script or the other, city or country.

What facets of your personality—of your likes, your drives, the things that light your fire—don't seem to match? And what are you telling yourself about that? Do you feel vaguely uncomfortable with it? Do you feel a pressure to pick a team?

I have a friend who is in ministry and can be the biggest personality in the room. To watch her in a public setting, interacting with people and speaking onstage, you'd think she was the most extroverted person ever. But here's what I also know about her:

she has an intensely introverted side. Like, after she goes out there and gives it her all in front of people and for people, she needs time to retreat. Time to read. Time to binge-watch Netflix. And it's not that the "public" person most people know is not real. It's very real. But her personality simply doesn't jibe with either of the simple labels of extroverted or introverted.

So what if? What if it's totally fine to be both a city mouse and a country mouse? What if it's great to be both extroverted and introverted? What if we don't have to choose but can embrace exactly who God designed us to be? What if we let him repurpose it all? It could make us more functional in our lives, in what we have to give, in the grace we can give others for their unique personalities.

What about you? Where do you feel like a walking dichotomy, like you're somehow wrong for not fitting a prescribed mold? What if instead of beating yourself up about it, you embrace it? What if, just what if, God knew what he was doing when he put you together, when he poured into you all kinds of flavors to come up with your special blend?

How do you know what's really you?

• • •

Every morning I pull on my sleek black rubber boots. I roll my hair into a big messy bun using only a pen or Sharpie to secure it. I walk outside into dewy air. I reach for my . . . shovel. Because it's time to scoop the poop from the coop.

It's a reality of raising chickens. They poop. All the time. Everywhere. They're appreciative of all the heart and thought and design I put into their coop, I'm sure they are, but they are not very particular about when and where they use the bathroom.

And so out I head to my doo-doo duty, whether I'm scheduled to get on a plane later in the day to go sing to a stadium full of people or head to my boys' school to resume my role as Super Homeroom Mom.

Here's why I do it: I love my girls. My chic chicks. I don't want them tromping around in a messy coop. I want them to be healthy.

And I want that for you and I want that for me.

Which is why, when it comes to the coops of our consciousness, that place deep within each of us that is how we perceive and understand ourselves, we've got to make sure to scoop out the poop of the noise and opinion and assumptions we sometimes allow to build up there.

For me, I allowed people to tell me that certain things were true about me. They often did it from a place of loving me or of wanting the best for me. There were definitely those who told me who I was, based on what they could get from me, or from a place of wanting to manage or manipulate me. I would take it all in, allowing it to bank up against the confines of myself, thinking they must know better than me or must see me more clearly. I would sometimes allow those opinions to be stored there out of a sense of wanting to be teachable, of wanting to be discipled, which are good things. But over time it got harder and harder to see the foundation of who I was created to be, what with all the chicken litter covering the floor.

When we get to that place, when the floor of our inner mental house is littered with all the opinions and acceptance and rejection of others, we've got to roll up our sleeves. Get down to the dirty work. Sweep away all the stuff that was well-intentioned, shovel up all the stuff that was just plain old mean. Get with that trusted mentor. Find that solid counselor. Invest in a couple of personality tests. Break out those journals from a few years back.

And most importantly, spend some time in prayer asking God, *Who did you make me to be? Where have I pushed away parts of myself that you delighted in putting there? Where have I not pushed myself like I should have, to help bring to fruition all that you intended?* Ask him to show you. And get ready to see him combine and validate and mix it all up in a way that you hadn't imagined before. Because he's all about repurposing all those facets he put in you so that you could shine far beyond your current circumstance, esteem issue, shame, or failure.

• • •

I've always been drawn to the story of Hadassah in the Bible. She had a rough start in life, born into captivity in a foreign country, those countrymen considered even lower than second-class citizens. Early in her life she was orphaned and was adopted by her cousin. Through all that turmoil, she came into a season of stability and grew up to be a beautiful young woman. She was cherished by her adoptive family and community and on her way to becoming a sought-after bride for some lucky young guy in her part of the neighborhood. And then her role completely changed.

The king of the empire began looking for a new wife. A pagan king. A king who didn't really know Hadassah's God, the faith of her people, her way of life. And a king who had ultimate power and authority in his kingdom. He issued a command that all the gorgeous girls of the realm had to come to his palace, where, after an extended time at the palace spa, the young women would be presented and he would make a choice as to who would be his new queen. And this command was not a suggestion: it was mandatory.

Hadassah's adoptive father told her not to reveal her

background but to put on this new role of queen candidate with wisdom and discretion. She stopped using her Hebrew name, Hadassah, and started using her Persian nickname, Esther. She quickly learned to network with the guy who had been put in charge of all the contestants in this high-stakes beauty pageant, and she learned to apply his guidance and coaching in all that training and exfoliating and etiquette for those twelve months of preparation before she was presented to the king.

Esther paid attention. She did all the things. Took it all in, learned it all, scrubbed and smoothed and perfumed. And when her time came to go before the king, he chose her.

Esther went from Hebrew girl from the wrong side of town to Persian queen, favorite of the king, all in the space of a year.

And then God repurposed this role in ways that were completely unexpected.

Scholars think Esther had been queen for about five years when her cousin, her adopted father, let her know there was a plot afoot to kill the Israelites living in Persia. Just as she probably had settled into the role of Persian monarchy, her Hebrew identity and its responsibilities came roaring back up, with an urgency and importance that couldn't be ignored. Esther probably thought that one quantum jump from anonymous Hebrew single girl to adored Persian queen was leap enough. But then God rewrote the script again and Esther discovered the real purpose behind her role. Esther needed to use her whole self, all that God had put in her— the humble and the regal, the slave and the queen, the obedient daughter and the bold wife—to save her people and find her truest mission.

So who was she?

Hadassah? Or Esther?

She was both.

She was the orphan Jewish girl. And she was the adored and celebrated Persian queen.

And God repurposed both of those facets of her identity to accomplish his purpose. If she hadn't been a Jewish orphan adopted by her cousin, she wouldn't have had the background and identity to fight for the survival of her people. If she hadn't been the celebrated Persian queen, she wouldn't have had the training and the influence to have access to the decision makers regarding the Jews.

> It's a breathtaking moment, to *see what God can do* with all those things we aren't sure fit together. But do.

She was both. She was all of it. She would have been none of it without the other. It's a breathtaking moment, to see what God can do with all those things we aren't sure fit together. But do.

• • •

I hear you. I get it. We don't want to be hypocrites or flaky or unpredictable. There's a big word to describe that. *Duplicitous*. It basically means to be two-faced. And I do take to heart the scripture that talks about being double-minded, because we should always be careful not to be all over the emotional map when it comes to our understanding of ourselves.

James, the younger half brother of Jesus and the pastor of one of the largest churches that has ever existed, in Jerusalem in the first century, warned about being double-minded. He wrote about people who pray for one thing but don't really believe in this way: "Such a person is double-minded and unstable in all they do" (James 1:8). So we have to make sure that in embracing those aspects of ourselves that don't always seem to match or go together, we're not actually stuck in a dirty coop of indecision and flakiness.

Look, let me mama-hen you for a minute. You can have both outgoing and reserved parts of your personality. And that's awesome. But if you're not following through on commitments you've made, if you're bailing out on your friends at the last minute, if you decide not to show up at that volunteer event you signed up for, that's not about honoring your more introverted, reserved side. That's about being a flake. And that's not how God designed you to be; he designed you to be a woman of your word. He designed you to be mature. He designed you to let your yes be yes and your no be no. So if you know you tend to sign up for things out of pressure, or you agree to go do something and then typically don't want to, let's back up a hot minute. How about you know yourself well enough, how about you embrace yourself lovingly enough in who God designed you to be that, instead of signing up for everything and then bailing, you pause. Just pause. Remember that you are unique. Take a breath. And then respond. Tell the person asking you to volunteer that you need to get back with them. Tell your friend who has asked you to go to dinner after a hectic week that you'll need to get back with her tomorrow with an RSVP. Honor both flavors of yourself *and* honor those around you by working with the personality God gave you instead of against it.

And let's get some clarity on this as well: Embracing yourself for who you were designed to be is not about making excuses for temper issues, dishonesty, or commitment issues. Those kinds of things aren't about your "personality." Those are sin issues, and you don't have to live by those. You can be free from them by the grace of God. They aren't part of your truest self. Shovel that stuff out of the coop and don't let it become some parasite on your personality profile.

I'm right there with you. In pushing through all the things I thought I was supposed to be and not supposed to be, I began making progress but also hit speed bumps. I would sometimes traffic in irritation and anger if someone was trying to put more on me. I would sometimes flake out, push back, be insincere.

The apostle Paul struggled with the same things. He wrote, "I do not understand what I do. For what I want to do I do not do, but what I hate I do. And if I do what I do not want to do, I agree that the law is good. As it is, it is no longer I myself who do it, but it is sin living in me" (Rom. 7:15–17). So, in learning to be thankful for who God made you to be, make sure also to pull on your sleek black rubber boots. Slick your hair back in a messy bun with a pen shoved through it. Grab your shovel. And let's get to scooping out what we don't want to be making a foundation of, you and me both.

• • •

Here's how well I know my chickens these days. I was recently showing a friend some of my girls' eggs. I pointed out a particularly beautiful chocolate brown one and said, "Oh, this one is from Sarah. She lays the biggest ones of my Blue Copper Marans." And then I showed her this Tiffany-blue one, almost round in its shape and small. "This one is from Hank. She had an egg get stuck one time, and I had to help her get it out. And her eggs have been a little odd shaped ever since."

My friend looked at me wide-eyed and said, "So you're now a chicken midwife as well? As in, you've gotten all familiar with that end of your hens?!"

"Well, yes," I said. "I guess I have."

It's all part of owning chickens. And the more experiences I have with these chickens, including helping them with stuck eggs, the better I, um, get to know them. I know what color and shape of eggs they produce. I know which of them has the highest egg production and which has the lowest. I know these things because I care for them and I love them and I provide for them.

So, yeah, the same hands that hold a mic for singing praises to God also shovel the coop and midwife eggs. Because that's how he designed me. For his purposes. For his glory. For his story.

And he did the same with you. In a fresh way. In a unique way. In yet another thread of his infinite story.

Flip the Script

- What are some things you've always felt were inconsistent in your personality? What would change if you saw them not as competing but as something beautifully repurposed and unique about you?
- Have you ever felt like you had to choose between two sides of yourself? Which side usually wins? Why?
- How would you say your friends and family would describe you? Which of their observations do you agree with? Which ones do you not agree with? Why?
- What are some ways you've seen God use an aspect of your personality as part of his plan?

Nine

Faced with Uncertainty

Bottled Up

I have this weird thing that I do.

Well, okay. I have lots of weird things that I do, but this one in particular, it's legit weird. Nic in particular thinks it's super strange. I'm not sure why he gets so weirded out about it. It's not illegal or immoral or expensive. I doubt it would make for any kind of embarrassing documentary. But I will say, I know it's a bit weird.

It started when I was a kid, on the road with my parents, driving from place to place, everywhere our home, nowhere our home. We'd pull into a new town, find the next church we were scheduled to sing at, get set up, do our thing. Afterward, we'd

137

stay as guests in someone's home until it was time to get on the road again.

After a few years of living the Honda life, we upgraded to a motor home. It was a light cream color with burgundy and navy blue striping bisecting its chassis. Talk about luxury! It even had the pull-out canopy thing, just like on a Barbie Dream Camper, so when we pulled up to a campground, we could slide that thing out and *presto!* create a whole other outdoor living-room space, complete with lawn chairs. It felt decadent and deluxe.

I stayed on the convertible banquette/bed in the front of the motor home, and my parents slept in the tiny bedroom in the back. Now we had a kitchen, a bathroom, a living room. We didn't have to stay with strangers or extended family anymore. We could take a few more items with us, a few more outfits, a few things that gave us a sense of place, even though that place moved almost daily. We had room to spread out.

We got to see all kinds of campgrounds all over the country. As we would travel between performance dates, we'd pull that motor home into the shadow of a mountain, or under towering pine trees, or into the vastness of a prairie. We'd swing a wide left turn into a designated campground, the hazy scent of thousands of previous campfires like incense. For a day or two, I'd have a yard and a view to call my own.

I became really good at making what I called Campground Friends. I'd find other kids also camping with their families and make fast friendships. We'd forge secret clubs and solve mysteries and swear to secret-keeping. I formed bonds briskly. I'd pack a year's worth of social interaction into a few days.

Most of these kids truly were camping, an exotic experience away from the predictable and safe routines of suburbia. For me, this was the most conventional domestic experience I'd had. Life would fall into a routine, with camp stoves firing up in the morning with the scent of bacon and coffee, unspoken but honored agreements about the rhythm of campground life. People would begin to emerge from tents and trailers at the same time each day. Kids would play tag and make forts. Our mothers would call us in for lunch and dinner. Campfires would flicker on like street lamps as dusk slipped past the sun. Routine, predictability, comfort.

Then my new friends would need to leave, go back to their suburban normal. Or I'd have to board the motor home for the next singing date.

Somewhere in this time frame, that's where this thing started. I can trace it back to the motor home days.

We'd be in a new town. We'd play whatever engagements or church services that were booked there. And then we'd take a little time to explore whatever city or region we happened to be in. I knew we didn't have room for me to ask for the usual souvenirs like stuffed animals or breakable figurines or anything like that. But I did figure out something that my parents would almost always get for me, something that seemed useful and like it wouldn't take up much space.

Lotion. And perfume. And any good-smelling beauty or cleaning product you can imagine. Portable, useful, purchasable in small containers. I gathered a population of balms and creams and unguents from across the country.

Here's where it gets weird. In Nic's opinion, ahem.

I would use almost the whole thing, whatever it was. But then, when it got down to the last couple of dabs or squirts or ounces, I would stop using it. And save it.

Because, what if I never went back to the place where I got it? What if this was my last bit of hanging on to the scent of it? The sense of smell, scientists tell us, is one of the strongest memory triggers for people, and it certainly is that for me. I could open a small bottle of some potion purchased years ago, and the memory of where I was with my mom and dad, and where we sang, and what the people were like, and what I did there, it would come back to me, memory wafting on the wave of a remnant in a bottle.

And that practice hasn't stopped even though now I have a place to call home and a house to keep up with and chickens who need me.

For all the clean surfaces and lack of clutter in my white-and-black house, there's a hidden collection lurking there. You might open the cabinet under my kitchen sink and see a well-organized space there with cleaning supplies that you would expect to find.

But I know the real truth. There are a couple of spray bottles of cleaning solution under there, in all that well-organized collection. And I know they've only got a couple of squirts' worth left in them. And I love the way they smell, and I know that particular scent of cleaning solution is really hard to find, and I'm pretty sure they've stopped making it. And so I'm saving it. Saving it for when company comes over. Saving it to remember by fragrance. Saving it so I don't forget, so I don't lose something, hanging on to the hands of the clock by hoarding a few ounces.

It's not just in the kitchen. It's in my collection of perfumes and lotions, laundry and room sprays. It gives me a sense of certainty in an uncertain world in which my favorite products get changed or discontinued. Certainty in an uncertain childhood where I never knew where I would be from day to day. Certainty in relying on myself, that I can stretch something out and resist using it all in an attempt to limit lack.

Nic thinks it's weird. Okay, it *is* weird. But we all do strange things to try to capture an aroma of assurance in a world that shifts and morphs all the time in this campground we call life.

• • •

I have a superpower. It's a gift, really.

I tell myself that I am Super Homeroom Mom. I'm determined to earn the cape. The Super Homeroom Mom cape. Because that's a thing, right?

Maybe it's because I only got a taste of public-school life before hitting the road with my parents during my childhood. Maybe it's because of the movies and books I inhaled with stories of kids in school and their desks and lockers and Trapper folders and Lisa Frank pencil bags. But I've got this whole romance going on with the idea of my boys being in school and me being one of "those moms," all into it and making Pinterest boards of teacher treats and holiday crafts and anything else that sounds scholastic and fun.

So this superpower of mine. More than the stage and the awards and the platinum albums, beyond whatever other accomplishment I may have achieved, I just want to be The. Best. Homeroom. Mom. Ever. Is that too much to ask?

And to be honest, I'm crushing it. I really am. Or so I'm told at least. (Here's where I would insert a *wink* emoji, if I could.)

Need something laminated? I'm your girl. Need an event planner for a Valentine's Day party who also needs to consider the kids who can't have dairy, gluten, sugar, nuts, or Red Dye #40? I've got you covered. It's hands down my favorite job ever, this room-parent gig. And it allows me to lurk and spy on my kids in a way that seems altruistic and helpful instead of creepy, so there's that too.

Because I spend so much time up at the kids' school, I've gotten to know the teachers and staff well. I'm thankful for the friendships and community I have there, an awesome circle of people all wanting these kids to do well and to love learning.

During Zealand's kindergarten year, I was at full throttle as Homeroom Mom. I arrived up at the school one day to see what task or chore I could help with, so as to continue to exercise my superpower. I walked through the door of Zealand's classroom to be met by his breathless teacher.

"Jaci!" she panted. "You just missed it!"

What? I thought. *What could I have missed? I'm up here all the time, for the express purpose of not missing anything. And to help laminate stuff, of course.*

"Two of Zealand's friends dared him! They dared him to do it! And then he did!" she beamed.

"Dared him to do what?" I urged. What was this daring thing? Were there broken bones involved? Streaking? Eating a frog? What?

She dramatically caught her breath, hilarity shining in her eyes. "They dared him to go kiss a little girl on the cheek while they were all at recess!"

"And?" I demanded.

"And he did!" She bounced on her toes at this pronouncement, kinder-romance making her giddy.

Okay, this was worse. Worse than frog eating or streaking. Pretty sure. Because . . . girls. My little boy kissed a girl?

I was half-horrified. And all proud. I know the math doesn't work. But I never said I was good at math. Because I'm actually the opposite of good at math.

But I'm telling you, that was the true equation. Half-mortified and completely well-pleased. Zealand, my little playground kinder-Romeo. What a player. Just like his cute daddy.

Kinder-Romeo. That would be a great rapper name, now that

I think about it. And it seemed like he walked with a little more swagger that afternoon when we walked to the car at the end of the school day.

But that feeling of abashed pride abandoned me later as I thought more about it throughout the day. At that point, we didn't have the official diagnosis for Zealand just yet, but we knew his path was going to be harder than most. That much we could tell, with his communication challenges and his difficulty with change and social settings. And because of that, this kinder-Romeo incident ultimately sent me into a tailspin of worry and doubt and uncertainty.

Here I was, trying to create the most stable environment possible for my kids, wanting them to have a school and a home and a *childhood*, those elusive things I felt I'd never had. And Nic and I were doing it; we were providing that. But then, Zealand's challenges, this unexpected turn, it was showing up and initiating uncertainty. So he kissed a little girl on the playground. And so began an entire avalanche of questions for me. What will happen when he's a teenager? Would he ever have a true first kiss? Would he ever get married? Have kids? Have a job? And what about a relationship with God? How would my very concrete-thinking child ever follow an invisible God?

It's like I wanted to bottle up Zealand, capturing this last whiff of normal before the next school year and the next and the next started. That's one of the things about autism that is so tricky. Kids don't really seem to notice anything about a child on the spectrum in the younger ages, in the younger grades. But with each passing year, the differences between Zealand and his classmates would grow more pronounced. Even in his kindergarten year, I intuitively knew that the slope was about to get steeper. We were about to leave this familiar campground of cut-and-paste, primary colors, and alphabet soup. The Campground Friends he'd made during this year were going to pack up and head into a different first-grade experience than Zealand. Most of them were going to coast into the next expected stop in their lives, while he was going to have to fight for every step.

And in my heart, all because of that little playground peck, I found myself scrambling again, desperately fighting the inner battle of wanting just one more whiff of the normal I thought we had created, wanting some way to put the coming change in a manageable jar.

• • •

I'm not the only mama out there who's saved the last remnants of resource and certainty in a bottle. Nope. There's one in the Bible. She had a jar of oil and was saving the last little bit. She had been married to a guy who was a prophet company man, if you will. I didn't even know there was such thing as a "company of prophets," but the Old Testament talks about it. These were men who would sometimes accompany a prophet when he would go to speak, and they would provide the music, singing and playing instruments. There were other types of companies of prophets as well, but it seems that perhaps this woman's husband had been part of a praise and worship band, Old Testament–style. Her husband had passed away, and this woman found herself trying to support two sons. Elisha, the talking kind of prophet, was passing through town, and the woman stopped him.

"Your servant my husband is dead, and you know that he revered the LORD," she said to Elisha in 2 Kings 4:1. "But now his creditor is coming to take my two boys as his slaves."

Elisha asked her how he could help, then he asked her an

interesting question. He asked her what she had in her house. She told him that she had nothing . . . except for a little bit of oil in the bottom of a jar.

Hmm.

Well, lookie there. It's not just me in the "save the bottom of the bottle" club.

Elisha instructed her to go ask all the neighbors for empty jars, as many as possible. And then he told her to start pouring that tiny bit of oil she had left into those borrowed jars.

I think that moment would have been so hard. There she was, with the last bit of what she knew was certain, that she had exactly this much oil left to try to provide for her sons. And Elisha told her to let go of it, to pour it out. But she did it. And that little bit left in that jar she'd been saving filled up the next-door neighbor's borrowed jar. And then the next one. And then the next one. And the next.

Verse 6 tells us that it wasn't until they ran out of jars that the oil, that little bit of oil that was left, stopped flowing.

So huge was this miracle that it paid off completely what her husband owed in Old Testament credit card debt, with enough left over for her and her sons to live off of.

But guess what? She's not the only mama in the Bible who was saving the last little bit in a jar. Turns out that Elisha's former boss, the prophet Elijah, had encountered yet another woman who had my same quirk. We read about her in 1 Kings 17. This woman was a widow and had a small son. God commanded Elijah to travel to this woman's small town, a place called Zarephath. When Elijah got there, he saw the woman gathering sticks and asked her if she could bring him some water. She started to go get that for him, and then he asked if she also could bring him some bread. At that point she turned around and revealed the state of the jug and jar she had back at the house. "I don't have any bread—only a handful of flour in a jar and a little olive oil in a jug. I am gathering a few sticks to take home and make a meal for myself and my son, that we may eat it—and die" (1 Kings 17:12).

So things were clearly bad. I'm sure she had tried to make that last little bit of flour and that last little bit of oil last as long as possible. And now this strange guy had shown up in town and wanted some bread. Yeah, right. Like I would have wanted to share with him.

But Elijah told her not to be afraid. God had told him that this woman would supply him with food and Elijah believed God. Elijah told the woman to go ahead and use the last of that flour and oil to make him some bread. And he told her, incredibly, that when she did that, God would make sure that the jar of flour and the jug of oil wouldn't be used up until the drought in Zarephath ended. The script got completely flipped.

So she did it. She poured out the last of that precious flour, she mixed in the last of that precious oil, and she made this strange guy, this Elijah, a little circle of bread.

She poured out what she had been saving as certain. She mixed it together with all that felt uncertain, but she added the most important ingredient.

Faith.

And God met all her needs.

That's how God repurposes our uncertainty and all the odd things we do to try to feel certain and secure. He asks us to tip it all out, not operate our lives from a position of feeling like we're on the edge of lack, but rather to lean in to a heavenly Father who knows all our needs. Who gives good gifts. Who has all the supplies.

I'm not going to pretend it's easy for me. I doubt it's easy for you either. But we serve an extravagant God who asks us to go minimalist in our reliance on things and the known and what we grasp at as certainties. And when we pour it all out before him, he shows up.

. . .

Nic has a current obsession with a particular Netflix documentary that chronicles the efforts of a couple of guys trying to embrace a minimalist way of life. They teach on it and preach on it. They take their wardrobes down to just a few items, toss out anything that doesn't play a purpose in their lives. They are teaching others how to live the same way. And Nic is an eager disciple. The guys on that documentary let go of household decor and extra sheet sets and that pair of pants that had been hanging in the closet for a couple of years and had dust in the pleats. Extra pots and pans. Memorabilia. Books they had already read and wouldn't be reading again. (Not like this book. You'll want to read this book over and over. But, you know, *other* books.)

Nic watched that documentary over and over, like it was a cooking show and he was trying to take down all the ingredients. And then he started listening to minimalism podcasts with a hot fervor. I guess you could say that he was ironically collecting minimalist resources. *A minimalism hoarder.*

Then he started applying it to our house. We had closets and storage units and a shed and a basement and a garage full of stuff. Stuff of all kinds. Premarriage stuff. Childhood stuff. Stuff from our single days. Stuff of the boys from when they were little. Stuff from our parents. And while I've always liked clean surfaces and unfussy decor, I didn't mind at all using beautiful white doors to hide all the stuff in the closets behind those doors.

Nic brought in black plastic trash bags. He didn't boss me about it, needle me about it, or push me. He just started, slowly and surely, to go through all his stuff. I started seeing him amble up the long hall from our bedroom to our living room, hauling a huge black trash bag behind him. He'd make his way to the front door, add the latest trash bag to a couple more he had in the back of the truck, and disappear to Goodwill. Then he would return home, and over the next few days, he'd add more things to more black trash bags.

Over time, week upon week, space started to show up in our home. Breathing room. His part of the closet was organized. Usable. He had his favorite shoes, his two best belts, the shirts he liked best. He started on the garage. Tools I'd forgotten we owned began to appear. Bits of projects that started out strong and never got finished began to disappear. Not Nic's words, but his example, began to make some noise in my heart.

Decluttering is a funny thing. At first, it's a rush. It's pretty simple. Anything that hasn't been used in a while, is out of style, or no longer works, it goes in the big black trash bag. You make a little progress, you see some daylight at the back of the closet, and it gives you a little thrill, juice to keep going.

But over time it gets a little more complicated. I've uncovered some things that don't seem to have a purpose any longer in my life but to which I am deeply attached. Like my boys' baby clothes. My boys are now ten and eleven, and my baby fever has come and gone. I'm pretty sure the fever broke when we were trying to get these two boys potty-trained and they were christening every bit of available drywall in the bathroom. So. Baby clothes. Could probably let more of those go.

But, oh my heart.

I'd done some purging in the past. When we were living

on the road, there wasn't much I owned anyway. But when the recording contracts started coming in when I was sixteen, my parents rented an apartment and I got my own bedroom with my own bathroom. The clothes started to pile up. The purses. The shoes. Oh, the shoes. A few years later, I bought my own house and furnished it top to bottom. Lots of those things stayed with me through the years, even when I got rid of a lot of things following my divorce and my move to London. And then there were all the sentimental things I'd gathered through my sons' babyhoods and childhoods, all the equipment and cutesy toys and all the rest.

But Nic's slow and steady decluttering started having its effect, and I started hauling black trash bags down the long hall from our bedroom to our living room and out the front door to the truck and then to Goodwill.

It was hard at first. It felt against my nature. It sometimes felt like I was being ungrateful with stuff God had given me. But most often I was worried that I wouldn't be able to replace what I was giving away. It would gnaw at me a bit, even though I knew it was silly.

But once I would make that step—take that pair of shoes off the shelf that I hadn't worn in five years and put them in the black trash bag—once I got through it, I discovered this funny emotion.

Relief.

Relief from the trust wrestling match.

That's what it is, really, this need to try to hang on to material and emotional stuff that we've had around for a long time and that we equate with being "safe." It's a wrestling match with God about how much we trust him. And when we finally release the object, the feeling, the last little bit in the bottle, relief floods into the space we thought would feel empty. That's how God repurposes those places we thought would be forever empty. When we clean out the meager and afraid, he fills it with what is possible and with his purpose.

I'm learning this, not just in clearing out my closet, not just in those little bottles stuffed under my bathroom cabinet, but in my fears and worries for Zealand. As much as I've tried to hang on to those little jars of normal, God is showing me that he's up to a much bigger story if I'll just empty out what my expectations and fears are. He's able to do much with my little—the little bits I've saved and am now learning to turn over to him. He's in the repurposing business, and I watch him take the dregs of my fears for Zealand and turn them into new vision. I watch him take the sediments of my anxious insecurities and turn them into greater trust. I watch him mop up the residue of my scrimping heart and expand my understanding of his goodness.

> When we clean out the meager and afraid, *he fills it* with what is possible and with his purpose.

And he will do it for you too.

There's a song I had the honor of cowriting with Aruna Abrams, Bobby Hamrick, and James Slater. It is so the anthem of my nomadic childhood, my search for the cure for uncertainty, the journey I'm on with Zealand. It's called "Trust You," and I think it could be your song too.

Flip the Script

- What are you struggling to pour out the last little bit of before God? Is it a relationship that you're desperately trying to keep bottled up? Is it a materialism that you think will make you feel like you fit in? Is it a position that makes you feel secure, but you know is not the thing God has called you to?

- What scares you about pouring it all out before God? What are your fears about tipping that bottle over and letting that remnant run out? Do you sense that God has been prompting you to let go of something? How has he made that clear to you? Is it possible that you could feel a sense of relief in pouring that thing out?

- Take a small step. In prayer, own before your God that you are struggling to let go of this thing in which you've put your confidence and security. Confess it to him. Ask his forgiveness. And then listen to what he says next.

Ten

Reno Rehab

Repurposing Isn't a DIY Job

It was the three acres that sold us on the place.

The house was sort of an afterthought.

When Nic and I started looking for a new place to call home, we knew we wanted to be on land. With trees. After leaving the slick downtown townhouse and test-driving a cookie-cutter starter home in the burbs, we knew the general area of town we wanted to be in next.

So when I found this midcentury-style ranch house angled on a huge corner lot, with an enormous backyard and room to run and trees towering up into the blue Tennessee sky, I was smitten. Sure, fine, the house itself had some issues, but look at all that land! Land, I tell ya! I was like a modern pioneer, knowing there might be some possible house dangers lurking, but so in love with the overall acreage and setting, we quickly plunked down our earnest money and started boxing up our belongings to make the move to the place that would become Velasquez Gonzales HQ.

We started out with some obvious improvements. First up, we put in a huge playscape for the boys, complete with awesome fort and swings and slide. We painted the entire inside of the house that crisp white that I love. We replaced some of the doors with these amazing vintage doors that I had found at a local antique place. But eventually, we knew we would need to focus some attention on the outside of the house. Because the outside of the house was sporting some serious ugly.

Precariously hanging on to the front of the house was this dilapidated deck that led to the front door. It reminded me of a bad costume party, when someone has applied fake bushy eyebrows and a mustache to their face, and at some point during the night, the glue starts to let go and one of those crazy eyebrows begins to hang sloppily from where it was intended. The deck had been painted a dark gray/black, contrasting with the cream-white brick of the house, and as the deck began to sink and shrink and peel, its pitiful state was made all the more obvious against the light background of the house. Amazonian-size shrubbery had been planted around the deck at some point in the past, and it was growing up under the deck, pushing through the flooring timbers and overtaking the railings with a *Little Shop of Horrors* kind of zeal. Nic and I tried to groom the plants back and reinforce the boards that seemed to be springing loose on the reg. But a scary-dark-jungle-sagging-ankle-twisting welcome to the front door of our house was not exactly the most hospitable first impression.

I was still working on the morning radio show and became

aware of a casting call for a show on the DIY Network called *Renovation Realities*. I thought it might be a good opportunity for Nic and me to show off our growing house rehab skills and also to give us an accountability kind of deadline for getting that eyesore of a porch-deck-thing taken care of. We put together a little audition tape on our home video camera and sent it off to the production company.

They picked us.

We were so excited and jumped into action to get our plan all put together. We spent a lot of time pricing materials and developing the new layout of the house. Since the home is a midcentury rambler, long and low across the front, I knew that a simple deck system with black and chrome steelwork would look amazing. It would give us a place to sit and enjoy the front view of the property. It would create the right kind of welcome for our family and friends. We put together our budget, determined the kind of equipment and supplies we would need, consulted with a friend of ours, Nathan, who knows a lot about construction, and prepared ourselves for when the camera crews would arrive from the DIY Network, ready to capture our super reno ninja skills.

We made arrangements for the boys to stay with family so they would be out of the way for three days, the amount of time we had from the network to pull down the old deck system, regrade the area, and build the new deck and incorporate all its new features. Things were right on schedule when the film crew arrived.

My hair looked really good that first day of filming. Really good. As in, a super good hair day—you know the kind I'm talking about? Where, for whatever reason, your natural cowlick is working for you and the mix of humidity and dry conditions is just right and your locks simply flow? That kind of day? And then to have film crews showing up at the same time?

Clearly, this reno project was going to be blessed.

Nic and I and the camera crew made our way out to the front of the house, and Nic and I began taking sledgehammers to the bizarre brick planter box that was incorporated into the sagging old deck. It felt so good to take that rectangle of steel attached to a handle and swing it into that planter box that had been driving me crazy ever since we moved in. The first few bricks fell away, and I started cheering like a kid at Christmas, the total vision for where we were headed seemingly so close with each swing of the sledgehammer.

And then we had to keep swinging. Because here's the deal with that planter box. I mean, maybe it was originally intended to be a planter box. But at some point, I'm pretty sure whoever built it decided it could also be a tornado shelter.

It just kept going and going. Brick after brick. More dirt after more dirt. The thing was built for some kind of postapocalyptic event, and I started to worry we would still be swinging at that thing up until the Apocalypse.

Hours later, we needed a different task to lift our sledgehammered spirits. Nic suggested we start knocking down the side railings of the deck. Yes! Now that was the kind of job I liked! One swing and the railings started flying off the side of the deck, collapsing like broken piano keys to the ground below. Progress! Discernible, honest, look-at-the-work-of-our-hands kind of momentum. It was a thrilling moment.

But it was just a moment. Like, seriously. Like, we knocked that part of the project out in just a couple of minutes.

We then turned our attention to the floorboards of the deck. They were a sagging, sad lot, snaggletoothed planks in a gray/black gaping mouth of lumber. We figured it shouldn't take us too long to strip them all away from the underlying beams of the deck.

We figured wrong.

We pried a few of the planks out. But then they began splintering. And some of them were attached to the frame of the deck with nails that seemed to be more like railroad spikes. *Okay, okay, a little setback, but we're prepared.* We'd rented a couple of saws for just this kind of possibility. We grabbed those saws, snaked orange extension cords from the garage to the construction site, plugged in, and got to work.

For a hot minute.

Until it started thundering and lightning.

At which point, it didn't seem too smart to be standing on an exposed platform in the pouring rain holding electrical equipment. But maybe that's just me.

We darted for cover, along with the film crew, and parked ourselves inside, moving to the living room to click on the television to see how long the storm system was supposed to last. Each severe thunderstorm warning that crawled across the bottom of the screen showed up as a time clock to me: we were losing precious hours for how long we had to complete this project. The film crew would only be with us for the designated three days, and I was determined, *determined*, that we would get the new deck installed in all its glory before they left.

So the whole Mother Nature PMS twist was not helpful. At all.

We lost several hours to the rain and then headed back outside, refocused and revved up. After a lot more sweat equity, we finally got all those floorboards up and were able to get the remaining frame down. Now it was time to tackle one of the great mysteries of the original deck system.

When Nic and I had initially tried to clean up and pretty up the original deck, we had cut back some of that crazy shrubbery that was overtaking the whole thing. And in the doing, we found something straight out of a Nancy Drew mystery. It was a concrete staircase. To nowhere.

Can't you just see the cover of the book for that one? *Jaci and the Secret, Pointless Staircase.* Me with a flashlight in one hand, microphone in the other.

The first few steps of the staircase had been completely hidden under all that foliage, and the rest of the steps were under the original deck. Some of the steps were covered in ancient green Astroturf, a total bonus to the entire randomness of the thing. The staircase didn't seem to lead to the center of the front door, and it disappeared under that crazy brick planter. When we were making our plans for the rebuild of the front deck, we knew all those aimless steps would have to be dealt with.

We were ready.

We had rented a front-end loader from our friend Nathan, who does a lot of remodeling and renovation in the Nashville area. On that front-end loader, we added a hydraulic jackhammer that we knew could make fast mincemeat of the mystery stairs. Or fast concretemeat. Whatever. You get the point.

Nic had been dreaming about being behind the controls of that front-end loader. He slipped on his cool black sunglasses, slid into the cage of the front-end loader, grabbed the handles like a boss, and got to pile-driving that crazy staircase. He looked like he was born to it. He looked like he was in his element. He crushed through part of one of the stairs, as I cheered like a deranged fan, the film crew capturing every nuance.

And then.

The hydraulic line to the jackhammer started hissing. And smoking. And the jackhammer stopped.

Somehow, we had killed the front-end loader, fourteen minutes into its maiden voyage.

Day one of DIY was a wrap.

• • •

When it comes to the things we think we're supposed to be doing and the way we're supposed to be doing them, it's understandable and natural to look at how others are achieving and want to copy them. You can learn a lot from studying how others do the things they do. I've got amazing people in my life who have shown me so much, from how to cook to how to decorate to how to pray.

But subtly, we can begin to take away a message from all that observation. And that message in my life has often played out like this: *If only I could be the kind of wife so-and-so is. If only I could write music like so-and-so does. If only I could just be more of this or less of that.*

And the noise of all that comparison begins to build and build until it can drown out the melody that is truly us.

I know that comparing ourselves with others is an age-old problem. I can even find evidence of it in the very first book of the Bible, in Genesis. Cain and Abel, two brothers and the sons of Adam and Eve, each gave God a sacrifice. Cain gave God some of the fruit that he had grown. Abel brought the fat portion of the firstborn of the flock he had been tending. Different preachers have different ideas as to why, but, for whatever reason, God really liked Abel's offering and was a little less enthusiastic about Cain's. And in that moment, Cain got trapped in the comparison game.

He was furious. Upset. Angry. God advised him not to base his emotions on Abel's relationship with God, but for Cain to do what was right in his own relationship with God. But Cain simply couldn't let go of comparing what he perceived as the differences there. He let the comparison burrow deep in his heart. He let it take root. He let it flower into a poisonous blossom.

And then he began to plot. And to scheme. You know how it ended. He lured his brother out to the field, the field where he had been growing things, cultivating and harvesting. But on that day, he cultivated comparison and harvested destruction. He attacked Abel out of a comparison gone wild and killed him. Yes, it's the most extreme example of "comparison kills." But still.

See, Cain had fruit in his life. After all, that's what he had offered to God. God needed him to do a little more work on it. He needed to work on giving his best, his firstfruits to God. But instead of digging more deeply into his own relationship with God and what God wanted to do in him, he decided to look across the aisle. To take a peek at his brother's paper and see what kind of grade his brother was getting.

And it drove him from running in his lane with his God to veering into a race of measuring and keeping score and envy. It was a race he was never meant to run. It was a race he lost.

In killing his brother, I'm sure Cain thought he was removing the thing he couldn't bear comparing himself with anymore. He probably thought he had removed the person he measured up short against. But Cain missed that it was his own heart, his own deadly game of contrast that had cost him everything. Ultimately, the book of Genesis says that God sent Cain out into the world, out from under God's presence, away from the land and the home he had always known, to wander.

While I haven't taken it upon myself to off a sibling in my life,

I've certainly compared and measured and contrasted myself to so many others around me. I've let jealousy and doubt and envy swirl across the windshield of my life, obscuring the path I was meant to take. And what happens to me in those times is that I lose sight of the fact that God hasn't designed me to be like the people I'm comparing myself with. He's already filled that mold in his purpose.

I want to be a lifelong learner. I want to keep improving. I want to test my limits and push myself and try new things and reach for more. It's good for us, you and me, to keep putting it out there, to keep striving to be the best versions of ourselves we can be. But right there, that's the thing: the best version of *myself*. Not the copied version of my girlfriend in the neighborhood who has the Instagram-worthy workout physique. Not the imitation of what the public thinks I should be or the replica of that other Christian singer. When the day comes that I get to meet God face-to-face, he's not going to ask me how well I did trying to clone myself off of whom I admired most. As 1 Corinthians 13:12 says, "For now we see only a reflection as in a mirror; then we shall see face to face. Now I know in part; then I shall know fully, *even as I am fully known*" (emphasis mine). I don't think I'll fully know myself until I see myself as God sees me, and I'm pretty sure that won't happen until I get to be with him in glory. But I can at least honor what I do understand of who he uniquely created me to be.

And you can too.

Whom have you been copying in your life? Did you start fluttering your hands like your mom when you talk? Did you start using a phrase because your best friend uses it all the time? Do you think you have to wear the same kind of clothes as the women in your Bible study? Do you try to do things the way your mother-in-law does because you admire her and, really, in your heart of hearts, want to be like her?

It's a recipe for jealousy. For envy. For feeling like you can't measure up. The realities of a heart renovation require us to remove all the stuff we thought we had to add to our front porch to make us welcoming and acceptable to people. All that stuff that has built up around us, like staircases that lead to nowhere and hiding places for spiders and wasps of the soul. We create a shaky platform upon which we invite people to "get to know us," when the real us is hiding, covering, copying.

> The realities of a heart renovation require us to remove all the stuff *we thought we had to add* to our front porch to make us welcoming and acceptable to people.

It's no way to live. It can't last. It will eat us up from the inside, or we'll explode on the outside and find ourselves feeling a long way from God.

Comparison is a game in which we set rules by which we can never win.

So we've got to refuse to play.

• • •

Day two of our DIY Channel's *Renovation Realities* started off well. Our friend Nathan brought a different attachment for the front-end loader. It looked like Nic was going to get to live out more of his Commander Front-End Loader fantasy and we would be able to finish up the demo of the deck quickly.

I sure hoped so. We were now hours and hours behind on our projected schedule, and we were going to have to make up some serious time to get the new deck foundations dug, cemented, and set.

Nic began digging back into the mysterious staircase. Until a horrible screeching noise sounded from the front-end loader. The big claw attachment that we had traded out for the jackhammer and hydraulic system came crashing down off the struts on the front-end loader, narrowly missing Nic's legs. I was praying and panicking at the same time. We were able to get the claw realigned and back on the struts. It once again looked secure, but as Nic started digging back in, the claw attachment once again looked like it was coming loose. I ran to the garage and found some rope to try to secure it better.

Okay, okay. It wasn't like a strong hardware kind of a rope. It was . . . curling ribbon. Like you put on a present.

Fine. Judge all you want. But I was just trying to troubleshoot as quickly as possible. We were losing daylight, people! We had time to make up for!

Nic let me know that curling ribbon, particularly sparkly curling ribbon, was probably not our friend in this instance. We then pulled out some black duct tape and secured some over the clasps of the claw that seemed to keep shifting open. It all looked anchored again and he dug back in, literally. And then the claw shifted again, the hinges popped back open, and the claw fell again.

We were done with the front-end loader. The possible costs involved, particularly to Nic's kneecaps, no longer seemed worth the supposed convenience.

We made another run to the equipment store and got a smaller, stand-up version of a front-end loader, all while the camera crew waited for us, our deadline looming ever closer.

I got to work with the small front-end loader, tearing away the final remnants of the weird brick planter, the remaining concrete of the mystery stairs, and the rebar of the old deck frame. I was quite proud of my demo accomplishments, until I almost dumped a huge chunk of concrete on my head. I've never been so glad to return something to the store as when we dropped off that second front-end loader.

At this point, we finally had the area cleared, a day later than we intended. But we were still hopeful, still full of vision for what we were going to build.

Day three dawned. Time to dig holes for the new posts for the new, modern, cool deck. We broke out the shovels, measured exactly where we wanted the posts, and started chiseling away. It was hard work, blisters bubbling on our palms. As the day moved on, I was so proud of what Nic and I were accomplishing. We got the postholes to the right depth, in all the right places. We mixed the concrete and poured it correctly in the forms, ready to receive the posts. I knew we would still probably have to work all through the night to make our deadline, but I was ready to do that, ready to prove that we had this in the bag.

After we got the concrete mixed and the posts seated, I read the back of the bag of concrete. It was supposed to be a quick-setting concrete. Which to my mind meant that we should be able to stick the needed post into its carefully mixed pool of concrete, give it an hour or so, and then start putting up the crossbeams to begin the deck construction.

But that concrete-wielding bag, it had some jarring information on there. That concrete bag's definition of quick-setting was different from Nic's or mine. As in, about a forty-seven-hour difference in definition.

As it turned out, this particular kind of concrete required a full two days, forty-eight hours of setup time, to be fully cured. I stood there, sweaty, strands of my crazed ponytail sticking to my face, mud all over me, letting this information sink in.

We wouldn't be able to finish. Not in the allotted time for the *Renovation Realities* show. Not in the time we were given for our segment. The camera crew was packing up the next morning and heading out. The boys were coming home.

And the concrete would still be wet. The concrete upon which the very integrity of the new deck would depend. The concrete that would serve as the foundation.

Nic and I looked at each other. And began to walk away from the cameras, a DIYers' walk of shame.

After the cameras packed up, after the concrete set days later, after all that, our friend Nathan came over. He took a look at what we had accomplished and what was yet unfinished. He looked over our plans and the materials we'd purchased. And he brought all his expertise and gifting to the thing. Within just an afternoon or so, the deck I'd dreamed of, the cool teak and steel geometry that would go with the front of the house and the white brick and the landscape, he wrestled it into existence. And it is beautiful. It's still one of my favorite parts of the house.

I felt like such a failure after the camera crews left. I felt like all the work we'd put into it, all the sweat and blisters and bug bites and near decapitations and kneecapitations by heavy equipment had been worthless. And then, when I looked at Nathan's relative ease at putting the whole thing together, I began to compare what a mess I felt I'd made with what a thing of beauty he created.

I had watched other couples succeed in previous episodes of *Renovation Realities* and felt that sting of not reaching the finish line. I worried we would look like idiots compared with what the other people on the show had been able to accomplish in the same time frame. I mean, come on, all we'd managed to do was tear down a teardown, if you know what I mean.

But I had it all wrong.

Nathan has a gift, a true gift for renovation. And he's added to that gift time and learning and skill. He's honed what he is able to do, and it really is a call in his life, to take buildings that are falling apart and to make them into something inviting and beautiful. And Nic has a gift. He really can work harder than just about anybody. He has some awesome skills at seeing the steps needed in a project and is fearless to dive in. And I have a gift. I have an ability to envision what could be and to apply what I've gathered from places I've been and experiences I've had.

So when I stopped comparing myself with other guests on the show, and when I stopped comparing myself with what Nathan had been able to do, I found something really beautiful there.

When we exchange comparison for cooperation, we can build. Build something beyond ourselves, build something that lasts, build something that celebrates all the gifts that everyone can bring to the table.

I've still got plenty of things that need to be renovated in my life. I've got sin issues I'm digging away at. I've got places I need to let the concrete set when it comes to trust. I've got my stuff and you do too. To be honest about what needs to be reworked, what needs to come down, what needs to be redesigned, can be good. It can be healthy.

But it means we cannot let comparison have a voice.

And here's what I've also learned.

I so badly wanted to DIY this whole front deck project myself. I took a lot of pride in wanting to show people what we could do. I wanted to succeed in front of a lot of eyes.

But there are times we need to reach out for help. There are times in our lives when what needs to happen shouldn't be a complete DIY job. It should involve a trusted friend, a counselor, a pastor, a mentor. Those are the people who have had the experience with the heavy equipment. Those are the people who've faced challenges in their lives before and know how to help us rebuild from a strong foundation. And so, there is a time to lay down our desire for DIY street cred and lean in to those who have been there before, who know the way and are able to share their gifts with us.

Now when we approach a new reno project on our house, I've got a new way of looking at it. I try to check the comparison game at the door and really dig into what we need, what will work for us. And then I get real honest about what Nic and I are good at and what we're not. And it applies not just to the physical house we're living in but to the spiritual house of our hearts. Because the realities of a reno, whether rebuilding a deck or a life, can be sidelined by comparison or strengthened by cooperation.

Here's the good news. Comparison is always a choice. And you can choose well.

Flip the Script

- What is an area in which you find yourself often comparing? Your marriage? Your waistline? Your finances?
- When you find yourself playing the comparison game, how does it make you feel? For me, I generally feel *less than*, like a loser. But I know people for whom playing the comparison game makes them feel better, because they play the game from a position of putting others down and feeling superior. What is it for you?

- Is there someone you learned the comparison temptation from? Do you come from a background where your parents compared how you were doing in school with everyone else? How did that make you feel?
- What do you want for yourself, for your kids, moving forward? How would your life improve if you could stop the comparison thing?
- What are some things in your life you would like to renovate? Have you been trying to do it solo, a full DIY? Who could you reach out to for help with some of the "heavy equipment"?

Eleven

The Great Repurposer

With Zealand's autism diagnosis came some answers.

And a whole truckload of questions.

One of the questions wasn't all that important in the landscape of so many unknowns. But still. Would he be a good swimmer?

Nic and I worked with Zealand and Søren in the pool, did swim lessons, talked about water safety, swam some more and then some more. We were grateful that both boys developed into very capable and smart swimmers. They both loved the water, bobbing in the pool, their matching wet dark heads gleaming onyx in the Tennessee sunshine. They both could dive for rings at the bottom of the pool, could float serenely on their backs for long stretches, knew how to tread water with ease, and could cross the length of the pool . . . and back . . . and forth . . . over and over.

But, of course, Zealand had his own twist on things. He would only swim using one arm. His right arm. He would kick with both feet but kept his left arm trailing at his side as he would tackle long laps through the pool. On land, Zealand showed no signs of weakness in, or resistance to using, his left arm. But in the water, it was a different story, and no manner of coaxing or encouraging could change his lopsided strokes through the water.

What was that all about? Was it something we needed to insist that he change? How important was it for him to use both arms over one? Were there other kids out there on the spectrum who did the same thing? Or was this a unique Zealand thing?

Over time, we decided it wasn't something we needed to fight. Zealand was good in the water and knew how to handle himself. That was the goal, right? So over time, we stopped worrying about it and just let the kid swim.

When Zealand was six, I was part of a movie called *Last Best Summer Ever*. I adored the director and his wife and their huge tribe of kids. Because we were shooting the film in Nashville, the director rented this great house for his family to live in during the movie production schedule, and when the movie wrapped, he invited all the cast and crew over for a celebration around the pool. Nic, the boys, and I attended the party. The backyard was full-on summer backyard barbecue magic, with spectacular landscaping and a wide, soft lawn with picnic tables and lawn chairs. Burgers and hot dogs were piled onto the tables and smoking on the grill. It was a beautiful, bright day with plenty of splashing, happy kids, and chatting, laughing grown-ups enjoying the setting and the celebration.

Nic was talking with one of the crew, keeping an eye on our boys swimming together in the pool. As he and the crew guy talked, he noticed the guy's young daughter in the pool. Nic pointed her out to her dad, asking if she was doing okay swimming. Her dad watched her for a bit and said she was fine, then turned his attention back to their conversation. Nic continued to watch her, something in his daddy Spider-sense giving him a warning. In just another quick moment, it seemed like she was starting to struggle. And in that split-second kind of moment, she was going under.

Nic saw that Zealand was the closest to her in the pool, and before anyone could say a word or even start running, Zealand took off like a shot, right arm like a blade cutting through the distance, legs kicking in rhythm. He reached the little girl before any of the adults could even comprehend what was going on. And he wrapped that left arm, that arm that he never used for swimming, *that arm*, around the little girl. And then with that right arm, that one he always used for swimming, that right arm that had been growing stronger and more skillful slicing through the water solo, he used that arm to swim himself and the little girl to the steps, where her dad plunged in to pull her from Zealand's grasp.

Scared and spitting water, she was safe.

All that time, right-side swimming had trained and strengthened Zealand for a water rescue far beyond the experience of his years and far beyond what most six-year-olds would physically be able to accomplish.

Just like that, Zealand's odd-duck swimming stroke revealed its greater repurpose. The thing that looked so lopsided in the land of expectation showed its grace in the reality of challenge.

• • •

There are lots of questions I have for God. There are things about him that confuse and confound me, things I don't understand, things that don't make sense to me or seem to fit. But one thing I do know about God is that he is creative. *Well, duh, Jaci*, you may be thinking. *He created the universe and the platypus, for heaven's sake.*

Yes, I know he's creative in those kinds of ways. But I'm talking about his creativity in the details and moments of our lives. That kind of active creativity that shows up after I've asked a lot of questions and have wondered over difficult things. And that kind of creativity of God isn't exactly some crystal-clear answer to the questions I've been asking, but it is this amazing ingenuity that shows up in an unexpected way and gives me a little glimpse of his bigger purpose.

One way he continues to dazzle me with his inventiveness is by playing a riff—in real life—where I least expect it. In music, you'll sometimes get to hear a riff. A song will be going along as expected, and then you'll have some amazing guitar player or vocalist just bust out there with this incredible improvisation. They'll shred on their instrument or wail with their voice in this way that completely brings out the heart of the music even though it's unexpected and improvised. I've watched audience after audience come alive when a gifted musician riffs in the middle of a song. It makes the music come to life, it elevates the whole room, and it makes the song seem alive and immediate.

That's what it feels like to me, when something I've grown used to, something that seems to be going along with all my questions and fears dragging in tow, all of a sudden has this God riff show up right in the middle of things, unexpected and brilliant. That's how it felt that day at the pool party, when all the concerns we'd had about the way Zealand was swimming one-armed suddenly had this riff, this moment of God creativity and purpose. In music, in a riff, it's not that the musician goes completely off the rails, playing a different song from what goes with the melody. It's that the musician uses aspects of the song—the key, certain repeated notes, certain tempos—and repurposes them to create this thing that reveals the song at an even greater level. And that's what I watched God do that day at the pool party. He didn't go completely off page. He simply rescripted what I already knew about Zealand, that Zealand has this crazy one-arm swim stroke, and then he made me see a bolt of brilliance and bigger story when Zealand rescued that little girl.

It was like I could hear the song of Zealand's life in a completely new way, all because God blazingly composed something I hadn't considered before.

• • •

Listen, I think some of the Bible-time folks get a little bit of a bad rap for not realizing who Jesus was. Before you get all ruffled, let me explain.

We sit here with the advantage of the full canon of the Bible. We've got our lists on the internet that show the hundreds of different prophecies Jesus fulfilled. We shake our heads in wonder that people didn't "get it" when Jesus was on earth, that they couldn't see all the ancient, amazing promises being accomplished right in front of them. I mean, there he was, born in Bethlehem, just like Micah 5:2 said he would be: "But you, Bethlehem Ephrathah, though you are small among the clans of Judah, out of you will come for me one who will be ruler over Israel, whose origins are from of old, from ancient times."

And born of a virgin, just like Isaiah 7:14 foretold: "Therefore the Lord himself will give you a sign: The virgin will conceive and give birth to a son, and will call him Immanuel." I mean, come on, what are the odds? And then there's all the genealogy stuff about him being born from the line of Abraham and Judah, and all that was fulfilled through both Joseph's and Mary's sides of the family lines. And that's all just at Jesus' birth. So many more Old Testament prophecies were fulfilled throughout his life.

But here's the deal. A lot of people thought the Messiah would come as a literal military warrior. A Navy Seal, if you will, swimming with both arms, churning toward the shore of Roman injustice and oppression, storming the beach and ushering in a new government. Instead, this guy showed up from a nondescript family, living in a nondescript town, with no money, no position, no discernible way to shake up the military and the sitting government. It was like he was swimming up a cultural stream with one arm tied behind his back. And that was not what people were looking for, not what they were expecting. He didn't talk the way they thought he would talk. He didn't look the way they thought he would look. He didn't tell them to rebel against the Romans. He didn't create a revolt.

And because of that, because they were interpreting the Old Testament prophecies about a Savior through a current events paradigm, they didn't hear the riff God was playing.

There are several times in the New Testament where Scripture says Jesus reached out his hand to heal someone. And it says in Revelation that he holds seven stars in his right hand. Some people think the stars represent the first early churches; others have different ideas about what those stars mean. However you want to interpret it, we know it means he has power in that right hand.

But here's what we can miss sometimes, just like a lot of the people living at the time of Jesus: When it came to saving us, he used both hands. Stretched out. On a cross. Anchored by spikes. On the one hand, the power to ask God to send a legion of angels to end his own suffering. But on the other hand, a submission to how God was going to repurpose people's understanding of the concept and the prophecy of the Messiah and expand it into something far beyond what they could imagine.

It seems to me Jesus was keeping that left arm at the ready to scoop us up when we were drowning in sin's riptide.

• • •

It was October 2015, and we were taking the boys to the Happiest Place on Earth. Which it can be, as long as you don't mind paying an arm and a leg for peanut butter sandwiches. It was the great Velasquez Gonzales Family Vacation to Disney World, and we were amped. We'd been planning and saving for this trip for a long time, and the boys (and by the boys, I mean Zealand and Søren *and* Nic) were giddy with excitement. We hit the park with a full battle plan, all kinds of ideas and tips on how to conquer all the rides and see all the sights.

But I was struggling. I'd had this weird crick in my neck for a couple of weeks, and the more we rode and walked and ate super expensive peanut butter and jelly sandwiches, the achier I became. At some point, after one of the rides, I felt like I could barely turn my head. Nic saw that I was struggling, and so we decided I would take an afternoon to get a massage to try to get my cranky neck muscles to calm down.

Off to the massage therapist I went, leaving Nic to fend for himself with the boys.

The massage seemed to help some. My neck still hurt, but I wasn't holding my shoulders up to my ears anymore in response to the pain. We came home from Orlando completely Disney-fied and happy tired, and I jumped back into my morning show schedule at the radio station and the boys' school and Nic's and my music travel dates.

Until August 2016.

I can look back now and see that things were building, but at the time, it really did seem to come out of the blue. I woke up one morning in unbelievable, breath-stealing pain. Pain that radiated from the hot core of the back of my neck all the way down my back. Over my shoulders. Waves of pain that would explode from that lava nest of my neck and send out rivers of fire over my whole body.

Nic somehow got a writhing me into the doctor and an MRI was scheduled. What that MRI revealed was that I had significant herniation and bulging of discs at C5, C6, and C7, which are the vertebrae right in that area where your neck and shoulders meet. C6 in particular is the spot where the nerve root branches off to create movement and control your arms. C5 is critical for flexibility and support of your neck and shoulders, as is C7. It's an area that can also be susceptible to damage because of the way we hold our heads and sit and turn to look at things and look at a computer.

And how we sit in front of a microphone. At, say, a radio station.

So, yeah.

Following the MRI, I was put on medical leave. I couldn't do any radio; sitting in front of the mic would make it worse. No talking; even the muscles needed for talking and the nerves of the throat were inflamed and upset by all the chaos going on in my neck. I was supposed to take it easy, get rest, and focus on avoiding the things that could further irritate and create more swelling and bulging of my discs.

The enforced rest I could handle.

The pain I could not.

Constant pain. Every breath. It stabbed me to slightly turn my head. It drilled my brain as I worked to keep my head still. Talking hurt. Getting dressed felt like razor blades.

And I can hear your next question, and I understand it, I do. *Why not just take meds?*

The meds scared me more than the pain. I've had too many people in my life who have ended up addicted. I've seen what that can do to people, to their families, to their careers. I decided not to drug up to deal with the pain, choosing instead to get by as best I could on ibuprofen and a heating pad. I know it's not the choice that everyone would make, and I honor whatever choice you have made if you've dealt with chronic pain. But for me, I wanted to get through this emergent season of inflammation the best I could without any more risk to my system.

Doctors were meeting and conferring to figure out what to do next. For a lot of people with my condition, surgery is the next step. But the surgery has a lot of risks for anyone, and in my case, even more. See, what docs have to do to reach where my cervical discs are messed up is to make an incision across my throat. Yep. They'd have to go in through the front to get to the back. Meaning, they'd have to cut right into the area close to my vocal cords. Those vocal cords. The ones I use to sing. The ones I was using at the time to be an on-air anchor in radio. Those vocal cords. And so that didn't sound like a great idea either. And my doctors weren't at all sure it would be the best approach for my situation.

Possible opiate addiction. And possible vocal cord damage if we moved ahead with surgery. Plus the uncertainty of messing with the cervical discs in my neck that control a huge amount of movement for my whole body. Plus my doctors not feeling too confident that surgery would work. So many lovely, safe choices before me. Not.

It took several weeks for the pain level to reduce a couple of notches. I slowly eased my way back in to work. But I had a new companion now, something that was with me all the time, in every moment, not shrieking per se, but always sounding: chronic pain.

It's still with me today. When I wake up in the morning, it's there in an urgent whisper. By the time I get to lunch, it's up to a dull roar. When the boys get home from school, it's loud enough to make it hard to concentrate. By bedtime, it's practically all I can hear.

Pain, pain, pain, a constant drip into the bathroom sink.

Living with chronic pain keeps you on edge. All the time. It's physically almost impossible to relax, because all your nerves and muscles are at high alert, at the ready to freak out if you move your head the wrong way or step off a stair at the wrong angle. And that means that your temper is always at the trigger. That your emotions stay thinly corralled behind paper ribbon. That your patience gets used up being applied to pain, so there's not enough patience left over to go around to things like work crises and kids and your husband. And chickens. Ahem.

When this all started, I had a lot to say to God about it. In those early, desperate days, it was just, *God, make it stop.* Then I moved to all kinds of positive confession, that I was healed, that everything was fine, that it was going away. And, believe me, I do believe in miracles. I've seen them happen. I've had them happen in my life and I know how to pray for them and hold fast and believe big.

But no matter what I was praying and confessing, this tangle with torment wasn't going anywhere. It literally had me by the scruff of my neck and was shaking me viciously, a wolf with a bunny in its jaws.

Then I started negotiations with God. If he would do this, then I would do that. I came up with some great terms and, I've got to say, God was going to get a great bargain out of the deal.

But it felt like he didn't even come to the table.

My questions to God through all these stages ran the gamut of *Why is this happening, God?* to *What did I do wrong to deserve this, God?* to *God, are you even listening to me anymore?*

But eventually, eventually, I stopped the monologuing and bargaining. And I asked the right question.

God, what do I do with this pain?

And then the answers started showing up.

• • •

I know there are a lot of people out there who don't have room in their theology for when things go sideways in life. Heck, I'd prefer a belief system that meant everything would go my way and there would never be one-armed swimming and neck injuries and inconveniences and tragedies big and small. I'd love for everyone to have clean water and a safe place to live. And if everyone could have a pony and a Tesla, too, we'd be in heaven.

But we live in a broken, broken world, and that means we live in a lawn of shards, the ragged edges of what could have been, shrapnel left from the explosive decision of Adam and Eve to listen to the Enemy and eat the fruit of the Tree of Knowledge of Good and Evil.

Dang it, Adam and Eve.

So here we are. Skinned knees, scraped ankles, doing our best to cross this treacherous field called life. And I do think God provides and shows us his favor. I do. But I don't think he's made us any guarantees to do it our way and to make it super easy. As a matter of fact, Jesus was straight with us, letting us know it's going to get messy sometimes. He said, "I have told you these things, so that in me you may have peace. In this world you will have trouble" (John 16:33). Um, thanks?

I'd rather follow a Savior who is honest with me than one who makes all kinds of assurances but leaves me hoodwinked when life hits. And while I'd like to write off the above verse as something he was just saying to the disciples, just a little job requirement kind of thing for them before they became the early church fathers, further reading in the New Testament shows that the Christian life, early church leader or not, has never been promoted as pain and struggle free.

The apostle Paul talked about the struggles he'd been through, that we all go through, when he was writing to the church at Corinth. He wrote, "We do not lose heart. Though outwardly we are wasting away, yet inwardly we are being renewed day by day. For our light and momentary troubles are achieving for us an eternal glory that far outweighs them all. So we fix our eyes not on what is seen, but on what is unseen, since what is seen is temporary, but what is unseen is eternal" (2 Cor. 4:16–18). And it wasn't just Paul who hit on this point. Jesus' brother James talked about the same thing:

> I'd rather follow a Savior who is *honest with me* than one who makes all kinds of assurances but leaves me *hoodwinked* when life hits.

Consider it pure joy, my brothers and sisters, whenever you face trials of many kinds, because you know that the testing of your faith produces perseverance. Let perseverance finish its work so that you may be mature and complete, not lacking anything. If

any of you lacks wisdom, you should ask God, who gives gen-
erously to all without finding fault, and it will be given to you.
But when you ask, you must believe and not doubt, because the
one who doubts is like a wave of the sea, blown and tossed by
the wind. That person should not expect to receive anything
from the Lord. Such a person is double-minded and unstable
in all they do. (James 1:2–8)

See, I used to like to read that passage in James for just the
"ask God and don't doubt" portion. As in, the Jaci interpretation
used to read just that portion of it as if God is a genie in the magic
lamp kind of stuff. But there's a really important word in there
that I liked to skip over. It says, "If any of you lacks *wisdom*, you
should ask God . . . it will be given to you. . . . When you ask, you
must believe and not doubt" (emphasis mine).

Oh.

Ask for wisdom. And don't doubt that God will give you
wisdom.

That's a little different from an Amazon.com-with-Prime-
shipping kind of a God.

Wisdom.

When I look at the story of Solomon, I see God's delight when
one of his kids, instead of questioning the situation, asks for wisdom regarding the situation. God was so thrilled when Solomon
asked for wisdom instead of position, ease, more lands, or money,
that he not only granted wisdom but resourced Solomon with all
kinds of other stuff as well.

So often, when we're faced with difficult things, with circumstances that bang us up and leave us stunned, we forget to ask this
important question. We're so focused on the why and the injustice
of the thing and the stress of it all.

But here's the request we need to make and then the question we need to ask, the question that changes everything.

The request: "God, give me wisdom."

And when we receive his wisdom, he can repurpose our questioning hearts, giving us new motives and interests.

So instead of asking, "God, how do I make this go away?" we can ask a question of repurpose.

Which is another way of saying . . .

"God, what do I do with this pain?"

· · ·

That's the question I finally asked about my neck situation, after all the praying and research and worry. I finally remembered to ask for what was needed most, the wisdom to know what to do with the pain I was experiencing.

God, what do I do with this pain?

And then I started getting the answers. Not necessarily what to do medically. Not an answer as to why I was going through this.

But an answer that repurposed, that rescripted my experience, one that allowed me to hear God play a riff in a song I thought I knew.

What do I do with this pain?
Lean in closer to me.

What do I do with this pain?
Seek out those who also are hurting. Invest in them. Respond to them with greater compassion than you knew was possible. Hurt with them.

What do I do with this pain?
Trust me.

What do I do with this pain?
Use it to sink deeper into the foundation of your faith.

What do I do with this pain?
Let it mature you. Let it teach you perseverance.

What do I do with this pain?
Let it make a difference. Watch me do it.

What do I do with this pain?
Bless it as a teacher, as a companion, as a friend who is reminding you of the suffering of my Son for the human condition.

What do I do with this pain?
Watch for my creativity.

God is repurposing my pain. I'm kinder now. I'm a more intentional listener. I move a little slower, which means I have more time to notice. I'm gentler with myself. I'm more empathetic.

And it's made me much, much closer to God.

Which means this.

I now have the opportunity to help bring even more people to his throne of grace. To share even more authentically the hope I have beyond this life.

From the pain of that first failed marriage, to the pain of Zealand's diagnosis, to the pain of my current medical situation, God can repurpose all of it as the Great Repurposer. And he generally seems to do that by playing a riff when things don't turn out like we expected, when it hurts more than we thought possible, when we face disappointment deeper than we'd like. And that riff brings hope and healing to others that we might not have ever encountered if everything was going our way.

It's not lost on me that the situation with my neck makes my arms a little weaker than normal. My right arm and hand are on my dominant side and have stayed somewhat stronger since I tend to use them more. My left arm and hand sometimes struggle against the pain to keep up.

But here's what I know.

Sometimes God has us swim one-armed so we can hook that other arm around another person and bring them with us to the shore of grace.

Because we've got a God who can repurpose everything, even those things the world would prefer be "fixed."

As that great philosopher Dory of *Finding Nemo* says, "Just keep swimming."

Flip the Script

- Where is a place in your life that you feel like you "swim" differently? Have you been able to use it to help others? Or have you struggled with being so focused on it that you don't yet know how to use it to help others?
- You may have always thought of God as the Great Provider, the Healer, the Holy One. And he is. But how does it expand your understanding to see him as the Great Repurposer?
- When you're faced with crazy circumstances, do you first request wisdom from God? Why or why not? How might

it change things if you sought his gift of wisdom first? And what would happen if you asked what to do with the thing that has shown up in your life, rather than asking how to get rid of it?

Twelve

The Ultimate Purpose

You'd probably think I was something of a lunatic. That would be nothing new, believe me.

But if you and I could be sitting at my long white dining table, slurping on coffee and swapping stories, for me to tell you this one, I couldn't do it from a seated position. I'd need to jump up and pace and wave my arms really big. It's that kind of story.

And it's probably the kind of story that can only be told if you're still decorating the inside of your house like a city mouse but the outside of that house is set in the country.

And by country, I mean . . . *country.*

. . .

Here's where a lot of my stories like this one start: Nic was out of town.

It's a thing with us. Some crazy crisis hits, and Nic is on a trip to sing or do mission work or whatever. I'm sure it's all noble and needed, but what I know in the moment when this kind of deal hits is that Nic-Is-Out-Of-Town.

Which leaves me as the primary adult in charge. Which is terrifying.

But let me back up to the beginning of this story, which, yes, begins with Nic being out of town, but also marks this little chapter in my chicken career.

It was not something I ever expected to put on my résumé. But here it is.

In addition to being a chicken mom, I have also been a chicken day care provider. Yes, I have been entrusted with the keeping and care of someone else's chickens. The guy who helps keep our three acres mowed down to a respectable length also owned chickens, but he was having some issues in his neighborhood, which was undecided on allowing chicken residents. He was waiting for a permit from his county office to allow his chickens to stay on his property. So as to not continue to ruffle feathers (see what I did there?), he asked if his chickens could come stay with me for a bit, since my Country Mouse county has no issues with chicken residents. I told him that would be just fine, that his chickens were welcome to stay with me while he sorted out their county immigration status. He happily thanked me, and we made plans that he would drop off his chickens the next day.

My chicken career was expanding.

He showed up the next day with a couple of crates, ready to add his chicks to mine. But then, controversy struck. My plan had been for his girls to stay with mine in my big, fancy chicken coop.

I wasn't at all worried that we'd have any kind of identity crisis. He had a couple of different breeds from mine but, after all, as we've established, I know my girls. So, I was just going to toss everyone in together and have us a little hen social.

But he hadn't just brought hens. He'd also brought a couple of roosters in the mix, and what that meant was that his chickens were all living in sin together.

If I wore pearls, I would have clutched them.

Now listen. My hens are virgins, and I intended to keep them that way. I didn't need some bad boy rooster strutting around my pure girls and being a bad influence. I'm a better chicken chaperone than that. This unforeseen situation of rooster frat boys entering the yard called for some quick troubleshooting on my part. Luckily, I still had my little chicken tractor and was able to move my friend's cohabitating chickens, the boys and the girls, into the chicken tractor setup, on down the backyard from what I was now considering my hen nunnery.

Problem solved.

• • •

The next morning Zealand marched into my bedroom, adamant.

"I never want to feed chickens again," he reported emphatically. "They are dee-gusting. Dares blood evawee where. Dee-gusting!" He was at an age where he would drawl out his *r*'s, sometimes making him a little hard to understand.

"What?" I asked, rubbing sleep from my eyes and pushing myself up onto my pillows. Zealand is a consistent and early riser and likes to get his assigned chores knocked off the list early in the day. He'd headed out early, like he always does, to let out and feed the chickens. And he'd often come to my bedroom after, to let me know how many eggs he found and that he was done. Surely I wasn't hearing him right. And I hadn't had my first cup of coffee yet, so all interpretation was a little fuzzy before that first caffeine hit. "What are you saying?" I asked again.

"Blood eva-wwwhere," he insisted.

He definitely had my attention.

"And dead chickens all over the place. I'm never feeding those chickens again. It's gwoss."

"What do you mean, dead chickens all over the place?" Caffeine deprivation was beginning to be overtaken by sheer adrenaline. Surely I wasn't hearing Zealand right.

"Mom. Mom," he started enunciating more slowly, since I seemed to be struggling with his message. "There are dead. Chickens. Everywhere."

I bolted up out of the bed, running for the back door. My girls! My girls! Genevieve and JoJo and Chubby!

I busted around the corner from the back porch at a full sprint toward the coop, heart in my throat. I ran up the hill in the back-yard to the coop, terrified of the sight that might await me. I came skidding to a stop at the wire door to the coop, my eyes taking it all in.

One. Two, three, four, five, six, seven, eight, nine . . .

All my girls. All present and accounted for.

All . . . just fine. What?

Zealand has a great imagination, but not in the vein of chicken violence. So what on earth could he be . . . ?

The other chickens! My foster chickens!

The living-in-sin chickens!

I spun on my bare heel and tore down the yard to the chicken tractor.

And there it was. Total chicken carnage. Five dead chickens, the chicken tractor door pried open—Zealand's assessment was absolutely correct. Blood eva-wwwhere.

Clearly, I'd had a chicken day care provider fail. In the biggest way. This was not going to look good on my résumé.

A fox had managed to get into the chicken tractor and enjoyed himself a fresh chicken dinner. And he'd left all the feathered scraps for us to find.

And Nic-Was-Out-Of-Town.

I started hollering the only words I knew to holler. "Mr. Howard?!?!?! Mr. Howard?!?!?!"

Mr. Howard is my neighbor next door. My backyard runs alongside his side yard, our acreage and his twining through the tall pines together. He's almost always in his yard or his garage, working on something, fixing something, chopping something, planting something. He's a true Tennessee "git 'er done" kind of guy.

He heard my holler and came ambling over, overalls and a sweat-stained sleeveless T-shirt his morning attire.

"Well, Jaci, good morning. What's the problem you got?"

"Mr. Howard, Mr. Howard, fox, blood, chickens, not my chickens, chicken tractor, for, blood, Nic-Is-Out-Of-Town," I blathered and stammered, still in chicken murder scene shock.

"Well, darlin', my goodness. Huh. Yeah, looks like you had a little fox git yer chickens. He done it good. Whew!"

I was beginning to be able to string sentences together again. Well, one sentence at least. "What do we do, what do we do, what do we do?!"

Mr. Howard rocked back on his heels, crossed his hairy forearms, and pulled on his chin, thinking. "Are you wanting to save the meat?"

"What?" I practically shrieked. "Ah, no! No, no, no! No!"

He looked a little surprised that I wouldn't want to take advantage of this unexpected poultry harvest. "All right then," he determined. "You got a bag or somethin'?"

Like a trash bag? Was this appropriate chicken crime scene protocol? Shouldn't there be some yellow tape and some finger-printing or something?

But then I quickly remembered that Nic-Was-Out-Of-Town and I had Mr. Howard ready to act on this chicken crisis. So I went and got a trash bag.

By the time Mr. Howard had the carnage bagged up, he'd arrived at another possible hiccup in what to do next. See, on our side of the street, the trash had come the day before. Which meant the trash guys wouldn't be returning for six more days. And this was in July. In Tennessee. So, I trust you can do the math on this one.

"So should we put 'em in your freezer? I mean, not for meat, since you decided you don't want that. But yer trash is gonna stink up something awful if we put 'em in there." He shifted his toothpick from the left corner of his mouth to the right, giving me some time to think. Which I did not need.

"No! No, no, no! No! That bag is not going in my freezer! No way! And not the trash can! No way! No!" I was almost back to the place where I couldn't form sentences.

"All right, all right," he soothed. "Now, I'd stick 'em in my freezer, but I'm full up with catfish and that five-point buck I got end of deer season. Lemme think, lemme think." He paused a moment, stroking his chin, thoughtful. While he considered, I excused myself to the kitchen. It was time for some caffeine, stat. These are not the kinds of decisions one should make from a noncaffeinated position.

By the time I arrived back to the scene of the crime, Mr. Howard had arrived at a plan. While our side of the street had just had our trash service come by, in that way that unincorporated neighborhoods in the country find themselves at the whimsy of weird school boundaries and school bus schedules and trash pickup, the houses across the street are on a completely different garbage calendar. Ours gets picked up on Fridays, but theirs gets picked up on Mondays. This was Saturday, which meant if we could, um, make a trash can contribution to the across-the-street neighbor prior to their Monday morning trash pickup, we'd be in a much better chicken disposal position.

Mr. Howard, God bless him, told me he'd get it taken care of.

I don't know which across-the-street neighbor received the bounty from the fox raid on the chicken tractor. I didn't ask Mr. Howard for details.

Some things are better left unknown when Nic-Is-Out-Of-Town.

• • •

The next day, Nic-Was-STILL-Out-Of-Town.

I made my apologies to my lawn guy about the passing of his chickens. He was sad but understanding, and I promised to get him some new chickens. Because, remember, you can order them online and have them shipped to your house or post office. So there's that.

Mr. Howard had checked my big chicken coop following the chicken tractor crime scene and pronounced it sound and safe, fox-proof in the wake of the day's events. But I was anxious through the night, hoping everything was okay.

Zealand got up before me, as usual, the next day, and headed out to the chicken coop. And then he came stomping back into my bedroom.

"Deegusting. Just deegusting."

What?!? No way. No, no, no.

I got to the coop, trying to ignore the empty chicken tractor staring at me accusingly from down the backyard. My girls
seemed to be fine, but they were acting a little odd. They were
huddled up together at one end of the coop, which is unlike them.
And they seemed a little nervous and flustered. I scanned the tree
line in the backyard, curious if they were sensing that horrible
fox nearby or maybe a hawk, but I didn't see anything. Zealand
followed me out to the yard, his manner very serious.

"Do you see it? It's deegusting."

"What's disgusting, buddy? What is it?"

"The snake."

Right then, I aged ten years. In that very moment.

Snake? I was in a wire cage with a snake?

"Dat's what I saw," Zealand reported. "I came out to feed
the chickens. It went into Genevieve's nest box!" Then I turned
slowly and caught a flicker of sinister, slick scales, coiling men-
acingly in the nesting box. Zealand turned around like a soldier
at Buckingham Palace and marched back into the house, his duty
done, leaving me to fend for myself. That turkey!

I was frozen for a moment. Because, really, what is protocol
when you've just discovered that you're in close proximity to a
snake and you're both in the same enclosure? If it's to freeze, to
not move, then I had that strategy down. But eventually, I figured
that playing the Lot's wife pillar of salt thing wouldn't be helpful
in taking care of my boys and getting breakfast going, provided I
survived this snake cage fight.

So I started hollering the only words I knew to holler.

"Mr. Howard?!?!?! Mr. Howard?!?!?!"

Nothing. Crickets.

I screamed his name a few more times, but only the sound of my own voice echoing off the hills greeted me. It was time for extreme measures. I told my brain to unfreeze my body and to run for it. Thankfully, my body and brain cooperated, and I dashed for the back door and slammed my way into the kitchen, peering out the window to see if the snake had chased me.

I grabbed my cell phone and punched Mr. Howard's contact info, stabbing the dial command.

"Well, hello, Jaci. How are ya this mornin'?" his voice rumbled across the line. I could have wept out of sheer relief.

"Snake, chickens, snake, big snake, snake, Nic-Is-Out-Of-Town, snake, snake, snake, help!" I urged.

"Well, Jaci, I'd love to come help ya. But I done cut my finger off and I'ma sitting in the hospital right now."

I think it's important for you to know that Mr. Howard has cut off three, maybe four, of his fingers in the six years we've been neighbors. He routinely hits one of his digits with a chainsaw or rogue tool or what have you. He scoops it up, puts it in the pocket of his shorts or overalls, and strolls on down to the emergency room. They reattach it, with varying degrees of accuracy. Mr. Howard has fingers reattached like most folks get their teeth cleaned.

This latest finger decapitation was very inconvenient for me. Very. Given the snake status in the coop.

Next, I called Mr. Professor, another one of my neighbors. That's not his real name. But he is a professor. Of something like super smart biology neuro something or other. I figured maybe the biology or whatever all his degrees are in might be helpful with the removal of an evil environmental presence. I'm not saying all my chicken crisis logic makes perfect sense. But, as I've told you, Mr. Howard was unavailable.

"Hello," he answered when I dialed, my cell phone sweaty in my nerve-shocked hands. I quickly explained the snake-tastrophe going on. "Well," he breathed, considering. "I'll be right over. Do you have a small shovel?"

A small shovel? Had I not just described a freakish python-esque kind of serpent invading the chicken castle?

"You see," he explained in all-too-calm fashion, "the humane thing, the thing that is best for the environment, is to rehome the snake. I'll just scoop him up on a little shovel and move him off further into the woods."

Rehome. I was all for rehoming the snake, right back to the depths of Hades where it had slithered from. I said as much to Mr. Professor.

"Oh, no, no, no," scolded Mr. Professor. "Snakes are good. They are good for the ecosystem. We don't want to harm the snake, we want to help it, and it will help us."

Blah blah blah.

Let me be clear. If you don't hold to my particular snake theology, in which it is understood that all snakes are evil, then you and I can still be friends. But you are wrong.

Very, very wrong.

I was desperate to get the snake out of my chicken coop.

And . . . you know the punch line.

Nic . . . was . . . out . . . of . . . town.

So. Limited options.

Mr. Professor tootled on over with snake compassion on his mind and I showed him to the chicken coop. The snake had decided to make itself comfortable in the bank of nesting cubbies at the back of the coop and had curled its inky black coils into a sinister spiral. As Mr. Professor approached the nesting cubbies, the snake started moving, possibly sensing a relocation was in the making. Mr. Professor gently lowered the shovel, attempting to slide it under the snake. I guess he expected that the snake would simply shift onto the blade of the shovel like it would become a magic carpet ride, curious to see where the winds might take him.

But no. The snake glided deeper into the covered nesting boxes, and we couldn't see him anymore. Mr. Professor was undaunted. He poked his head into the nearest nesting box to figure out where the snake had gone. Now, it's dark in those nesting boxes. I personally would have to question the sanity of anyone boldly jamming their head into that space after a recent snake sighting. But who am I to judge, as long as I'm not the one having to do it?

Mr. Professor called to me in a muffled voice from inside the box, "I'm having trouble seeing where he went, Jaci! Can you hand me your phone with the flashlight on?" I didn't know until that moment that I actually have a strong belief system about my phone and snakes. My phone should not be anywhere near a snake. As it turns out, I have a strong ethic about this.

But, again, Nic-Was-Out-Of-Town and Professor Earth Lover was my best bet at this point. And the man needed my phone.

And since I didn't want to come any closer than necessary to the nesting boxes, I leaned over as far as possible from my perch near my escape hatch at the door of the coop, and handed over my cell phone, flashlight on.

Mr. Professor palmed the phone in one hand, gripping the shovel with the other. He shoved his head back into the nest, bringing the phone up by his cheekbone, searching for the snake. He twisted and turned, looking all around. He backed up, brought the shovel back up, attempted again to gently encourage the snake to board the shovel blade willingly. The snake disagreed, a little more forcefully this time, swirling farther into the depths of the nest.

Mr. Professor was starting to get a little frustrated. It's a pain when nature doesn't do what humans want.

He dived back into the coop again, cell flashlight at the ready . . . and promptly dropped my cell phone into the depths of chicken poop and feathers at the bottom of the roosting stack.

Just lovely.

The snake hissed and slithered and slipped ever deeper into the gloom. Mr. Professor was starting to get a little sweaty and red.

They continued this dance for a long time, Mr. Professor trying to preserve wild nature, the snake determined to inhabit tamed chicken habitats because . . . free eggs. Mr. Professor was getting angry, and the snake was past angry. If I hadn't been so creeped out by the snake, I would have almost enjoyed the show.

This is the part where those of you who don't share my snake theology need to just skip ahead to the next section. Go ahead. Go on now. I'll see you over there in a few minutes.

For the rest of you theologically sound people, here's the rest of the story.

Mr. Professor finally hit the end of his need to humanely rehome this reptile, exited the coop, and returned with a BB gun, whereupon the snake was briskly rehomed to the pit of Hades from where it had come.

All while Nic-Was-Out-Of-Town.

• • •

All these crazy stories in my life. And all the crazy stories in yours. The funny ones, the weird ones, the sad ones, the awful ones, the joyful ones, the unexpected ones, the predictable ones—those stories are the makings of us. They are how we understand ourselves, how we place ourselves in the world. When I think about the various stories in my life, the ones that make me laugh, the ones that make me cry, the ones that make me angry, the ones that make me proud, I often think of each of them as singular events. But when I back up a bit, when I refocus the eyes of my heart, a lyric begins to emerge. Things I thought of as isolated incidents begin to connect, begin to form a melody.

Do you feel like that, like you've got random events in your life, these individual stories? Can I just tell you: they're adding up to something. It's not always clear, it's not always obvious, but God is in there, stringing all those events and anecdotes and comedies and tragedies and histories together. Your life has a fuller story to tell, and God will connect all those dots, all those points of experience as you live out your days.

Through all of it, all the experiencing, all the retelling, God is up to one thing—one ultimate purpose.

He wants you to know something, to know it so deep down to your core that you can see it in every angle, every note of each moment of your life that plays out.

What he wants you to know is this: you are his child. His. Wanted, loved, designed, specifically placed in time as his.

What he wants you to do with this knowledge is this: to live as his child fully in this day, to be transformed into his spiritual image, fully who he created you to be and fully redeemed.

I used to think of the things that happened to me as random bits of good decisions and bad ones, happy days and sad ones, times I got it right and times I got it wrong.

But your life is not random to God. It's ransomed.

There was a time I wouldn't have understood why a fox would take down my chicken tractor. Why God would move me next door to Mr. Howard. Would move me down the street from Mr. Professor. Why Nic would be out of town while chicken mayhem ensued.

I'm certainly not claiming I totally see it all now.

But here's what I do know. All of it, it's part of a bigger book God is writing, the message he writes over and over to you and to me, that we are his, treasured, loved.

God tells the most amazing stories. After all, he is the author of the greatest story ever told. And he's willing to work with all kinds of material: The stuff I'm proud of, the stuff I'm not. The failures, the progress, the two steps forward, the one step back.

I mean, look at all the factors that had to go into the fox and the snake and the neighbor adventures. There's nothing random about it. First, he created the beautiful Tennessee countryside and created a piece of land that would capture Nic's and my hearts as the place to raise our family. God led us to move to that certain neighborhood, with people next door and down the street who are also his children, with their own gifts and skills, people who are willing to come running when I call. He designed chickens. And foxes. And, it pains me to say it, snakes. He created summer mornings and chores and fresh eggs, and he blends it all together with storylines that make me appreciate my neighbors and love my chickens and find him in the hilarious moments and in the crises.

In small ways and big, he's always showing me there is a bigger picture going on than just the day-to-day scenes of my life.

What if?

What if you let him into your story? What if you opened your heart to letting him show you that everything you experience, the things you wish you could take back, the things you count as your best days, the things that you regret, the things that weren't fair, the things that were deliriously awesome, what if you could pull the lens back and see it all as a beautiful mosaic, a story he's building to completion?

In that time I spent in London, I'd troll some of the various old cathedrals. The ancient stone, the pillars, the pews, the incense, the quiet, it made for contemplative settings. And the stained glass always drew me in. I'd stand before a massive window and look at all the tiny squares of colored glass. Here a circle of red. There a shard of green. Over here a pane of blue. Those individual pieces are important, carefully crafted and placed. Some of them were my favorite colors. Some were not. But then I would back up. Look up. Crane my neck. And move my vision from the individual panes of glass to the larger story.

There it would be. A story told in glass of someone from the Bible or of a saint's sacrifice in the early days of the church. All those bits of glass I could now see for their ultimate purpose, once I backed up and allowed the total story to come into view. And all those mosaics were recounting the life of a person who mattered to God. The God who has the ultimate purpose in mind, that each of us would be drawn to him, would receive his redemption and salvation, would fulfill all the days he has written for us.

> The *details* of your life matter because they make up the *total story* of your life.

The details of your life matter because they make up the total story of your life. Yes, you may have chapters that are huge in your story. You may have chapters that seem less important. You may have chapters that tell of a devastation. But you're still here. The story isn't over. The thesis remains the same: You matter to God. You live as his child. And that is the ultimate purpose of his story for you. That's the artistry of what God does, repurposing everything that happens to you and everything you do to be crafted into a greater story. That's the ultimate art of repurposing.

• • •

After the great chicken tractor raid, after the snake-ageddon incident, after Mr. Professor had dispatched the serpent and I'd calmed my girls and made peace back in the coop, I pushed open the back door to the house, kicking off my muddy rain boots at the threshold. I had two things on my mind: coffee and a shower. I pulled the sunglasses off the top of my head, pulled my keys from one pocket, my recovered (and somewhat still chicken-poop-smudged) cell phone from the other, and tossed them onto the sewing machine cabinet next to the door.

That sewing machine cabinet.

That awkward hand-me-down that I never thought would fit in my home, my decor, my plan, my brand. That thing that I could have cast off because I thought it didn't have a place in my life. Yet there it was—repurposed, redeemed, needed, and appreciated in the context of my daily life. That cabinet holds the story of my mother-in-law's early married life. It holds the story of Nic's boyhood. Now it's holding the stories of the generation Nic and I are building in Søren and Zealand. It's where I toss my keys after an average day. It's where I toss my keys after days that require Mr. Howard. And Mr. Professor.

And I could have missed what it would come to mean, had God not shown me the art of repurposing.

I want you to come away from our time together with this going deep down into your heart: You matter. You matter to God. Don't let a detail that doesn't seem to fit with what you expected in your life be the only focus. Repurpose that pain. See that detail with fresh eyes. Put a new lens on it. Embrace the personality you were gifted with and let the Holy Spirit repurpose the parts of you that you haven't been so sure were valuable. Don't decide it's too late. Let God run the clock. You have so many more beautiful chapters in your story. Trust him with every nuance, every element. Let him repaint, refurbish, renew, and redeem.

And let God repurpose it all to draw you close to him.

We know that in all things God works for
the good of those who love him, who have
been called according to his purpose.

ROMANS 8:28

Acknowledgments

God, my Father, your Son, and the Holy Spirit—I am humbled and in awe to be called your daughter.

My better half, Nicolas (Bobs), your love has painted the most beautiful picture of what it looks like when he says, "Husbands, love your wives, just as Christ loved the church and gave himself up for her." (Eph. 5:25 NIV)

Zealand, my oldest, you singlehandedly taught me what love at first sight was, and you continue to do so daily.

Søren, my baby, your heart teaches all of us just how good humanity can be. I don't know what God has for you, but it's gonna be so incredibly special.

Nana and Tata, you have always stood, and still stand in the gap. Thank you, we love you and don't know what we would do without you.

Grandpa David and Grandma Cathy, we love you.

Momo and Popo—never get old, never die. You both have to stay alive forever!

Julie, you are superhuman, thank you for your friendship and your amazing family.

Greg, thank you for pushing me, believing in me, and being a friend.

Jenny, it's amazing how sometimes we feel like an island, but it's beautiful to know that WE are not alone on this earth, there are others that have stories that mirror our own.

Laura, Glyna, and Sherry—our babies' stories are STILL being written and they are gonna be epic!

My kids' teachers and future teachers, paraprofessionals, file holders, principals, vice principals, and therapists—you have taught me so much. I'm amazed at the patience you have not only for the kids, but the parents as we try to navigate uncharted territories. You are so appreciated.

To the beautiful and lovely ladies of FEDD, y'all are amazing!

To the Thomas Nelson posse, thank you ALL for your excitement, belief, and support. Excited to see this book get into the hands that God wants.

To every mom, dad, sibling, family, and person that has been given very special children: our timing is not God's timing. His plan is perfect. It is also completely okay to ask, *Why?* He may not answer how you think He should but remember this: "We all experience times of testing, which is normal for every human being. But God will be faithful to you. He will screen and filter the severity, nature, and timing of every test or trial you face so that you can bear it. And each test is an opportunity to trust him more, for along with every trial God has provided for you a way of escape that will bring you out of it victoriously." (1 Cor.10:13 TPT)

Notes

1. Google Dictionary, s.v. "flip the script," accessed April 22, 2019, https://www.google.com/search?q=Dictionary#dobs=flip%20 the%20script.
2. Online Etymology Dictionary, s.v. "role," accessed April 22, 2019, https://www.etymonline.com/search?q=role.
3. Sandi Greene, "When Your Parents Divorce," Boundless, March 17, 2011, https://www.boundless.org/relationships/when-your -parents-divorce/.
4. Michael Foust, "Christian Music Star Velasquez Criticized for Scenes in New Movie," Baptist Press, April 24, 2003, http://www .bpnews.net/15788/christian-music-star-velasquez-criticized -for-scenes-in-new-movie.
5. Andree Farias, "Latin Lovebirds," Crosswalk.com, May 12, 2008, https://www.crosswalk.com/11618146/.

About the Author

Jaci Velasquez has attained three RIAA certified Platinum albums, three RIAA certified Gold albums, sixteen No. 1 singles, six more singles in the top 10, seven Dove Awards, three Latin Grammy Award nominations, and three Grammy Award nominations. She has also graced more than fifty magazine covers, including *Teen People*, *Latin Girl*, *Teen Beat*, *Parade*, and *People* and has appeared in ads for Pepsi, Doritos, and Target. For nearly six years, she has cohosted Salem Broadcasting Network's "The Family Friendly Morning Show with Doug and Jaci Velasquez" with more than 1.5 million daily listeners. In addition to writing, recording, touring, and serving as an advocate for autism awareness, Velasquez has been featured in five faith-based films since 2009, hosted the SESAC Christian Music Awards and the GMA IMMERSE conference, and has been internationally active in the music industry since her emergence as an award-winning artist at the age of sixteen.